A Journey Back To Me

A Tale Of Trauma And Triumph
By Eboni Davis

Ignited Ink 717
2020

Copyright © 2020 Eboni Davis
All rights reserved. This book or any portion thereof may not be re-produced or used in any manner whatsoever without the express written permission of the publisher except for the use of brief quotations in a book review or scholarly journal.

First Printing: 2020
ISBN 978-1-7352286-3-1
www.whoAmiInc.org

Ignited Ink 717
IgnitedInk717@gmail.com
@IgnitedInk717

Acknowledgements

Gee Gee Brown (A dear friend)
Arbrelia Davis (mother)
Lee Davis (father)
Ann Jackson (grandmother)
Dave Jackson (grandfather)
Grandmother & Grandfather (RIP)

Thank you for grounding me in church. Although I strayed, it has all come back full circle. I'm radically sold out for God. Love you.

Mother

I've tried so long to make it without you, but the truth is I really do need you. We can no longer stand divided. I am you—you are me. We can't change the past. However, we can accept it and move into our future as mother and daughter. Mom, I appreciate you. Please forgive me as I have forgiven you.

Foreword: Who Am I?
A Journey Back To Me

Like me, many believers in the Christian faith transition into their spiritual walk from a place of deep pain and regret. For some, after they receive their forgiveness and commune with God, they either intentionally or unintentionally bury the details of their former selves. While this desire is understandable, it is just as important to me to remain grounded by being open. Therefore, out of respect to my fellow Christians, I forewarn that the contents of this book will not model many of the precepts of Christian practice and may be defined as explicit. It is the story of my personal truth and the discovery of who I am. It details the spiritual and emotional journey back to rescue the child inside, who was lost and damaged long ago. I assure all readers that, regardless of what I share here, I am a believer in our Lord Jesus Christ who is the author and finisher of all my writings.

I was inspired to write this book to find healing in myself and hopefully help others do the same. I always used to wonder why all this unfortunate stuff happened to me and why I had to experience it. As I look back, I am thankful and recognize the blessing through trials. Of all the horrendous experiences, I also see that it was as if, despite all things, I had a hedge of protection around me. As I have gotten older, I have gained wisdom enough to know you don't have to be haunted by family curses, strongholds, or dysfunction. May you gain the same realization as I share what are no longer my deep, dark secrets with you in a creative way. This book is primarily based upon events I have witnessed or endured. Some portions have been modified through interlacing of the fiction genre. All readers should bear in mind that similarity in stories does not necessarily mean it is the same story. Any resemblance to persons, businesses and events may be purely coincidental. As has been foretold, there is nothing new under the sun.

Épigraphe

If you ain't never gone through something, you ain't got nothing to talk about!

Table Of Contents

Chapter One	1
Chapter Two	37
Chapter Three	44
Chapter Four	58
Chapter Five	63
Chapter Six	83
Chapter Seven	104
Chapter Eight	120
Chapter Nine	130
Chapter Ten	151
Pieced Together	164
Bonus	167

Chapter One
Haunted By My Inner Child

"Get the fuck out of my house!"

Time stood still. I turned away from our game of jacks to see what caused my mother to yell such a thing. The jagged pieces dropped from my hand, unheard amongst the chaos. The ball bounced down the road, chasing my mother, as she chased after my father, hurling canned vegetables at him. He ducked and dodged the first two, but was not so lucky the third time. A can of family-sized corn hit him in the center of his back with great force. He paused in agony before hopping into his pick-up truck. My siblings and I puzzled together over the bizarre events we were witnessing. That night, we would bond over sobs and fear.

"You crazy bitch!" he yelled as he slammed the door and started the engine. "You aren't even half the woman she is. Good riddance!"

The tires screeched as he sped off, turning our small neighborhood into NASCAR. At the tender age of seven, I tried to understand the missing pieces of my puzzle. I was too young to understand the word 'affair', but soon I would understand first-hand.

'Affair' became synonymous with the second-rate family that just wasn't good enough for my father. The smell of burnt rubber started the trail to my dad's newest offspring. It is difficult to connect now to the time I believed my life was a thing of purity and beauty. The time that was laced with innocent giggles and freedom. In this phase, we are ignorant of how today will affect our tomorrow. If you talk to anyone else, they may give you a different recollection of my life.

They would tell you about all the material things my family possessed. They would speak of how I was happy, using home videos as evidence. In them can be seen a beautiful home, an attractive mother who was a housewife, an accomplished stern father who was a police officer, and children as perfect and blessed as can be. Of course, my actions corroborated this picture of contentment. I easily greeted people in my life with my plastic smile and modeled what it was to be okay.

I suspect they never paid attention to the emptiness in my eyes. They missed the pain-induced anger bubbling within me, just waiting to spill over and poison my surroundings. I began to believe the facade. My mind's survival mode suppressed the memories that would reveal the severity of my scars. But the moments came rushing back in as I read the letters.

When my maternal grandmother passed away in 2009, my sister shared a box of notes with me that she had found in one of my grandmother's shoeboxes. The box contained years' worth of letters my mom wrote to my grandmother concerning my behavior. Letter after letter declared me to be a handful. One letter delivered the ultimatum that, if my grandmother did not take custody of me, I would become a child of the state.

Imagine being an adult dealing with the death of your grandmother, while trying to digest harsh words found in dozens of letters from your own mother. However, let us not skip too far ahead. This journey truly begins when I was seven, with the breakup of my parents.

I was introduced to another vocabulary word to master the meaning of: divorce. As an upper-middle-class family, the divorce proceedings were formal and legally driven, focusing on capital and property. The divorce was long and drawn-out, but that wasn't what hurt most. My father's actions and choices showed me that the love I carried for him wasn't mutual. Forget any visions I had of possibly living with him and his new family. That was never a part of his plan. My dad removed all his belongings from our home shortly after screeching away.

My parents often had 'meetings' that were none of our concern. It was grown folks' business that we needed to stay out of. They spent most of that 'meeting' time arguing and threatening each other. There was a time when my father seemed to be coming around to wanting us. He had agreed to pick us up to spend time with us. We were in the living room playing when he arrived.

"Are your things ready?" my dad asked.

As the eldest, I answered for all of us, oozing our collective enthusiasm. At that moment, my mom appeared. The light beaming through the window made her summer dress slightly translucent. I could see the shadow of her hourglass curves. She tilted her head and the tendrils of her hair cascaded on her shoulder. She parted her deep plum-painted lips and smiled before calling me to her, while my father glared at her with a silence that could make the hair stand up on the back of your neck.

"Be a good girl this weekend. Take good care of your brother and sister," my mom said. She leaned close to my ear and whispered, "Remember, you only have one Mama. If that bitch mistreats you in any way just call me. Your Uncle Mike and I will be there in a flash."

Satisfied with her private message, she sent me off to collect our things. As I disappeared out of the room, I heard him ask her, "What are you all fixed up for?"

"None of your damned business, motherfucker!" she blurted.

I tried to quickly gather our things. I hated it when she talked that way. I didn't want to hear another of their blowouts. While scurrying around getting our toys, I realized I didn't have my brother's bear. If he didn't have it at bedtime, he would cry for hours before falling asleep. I didn't want to hear that either. So, I started looking all over the place. I heard some strange bumping around in the living room, but had no time to focus on it as I started pulling every toy out of his chest and from under the beds. Empty-handed, I left the room. I remembered he had slept with our mom the night before, so his bear was probably in her bed.

I ran into my mom's room as if I was in a playground, but stopped in my tracks. I was stunned. My dad's pants were pulled to his thighs, he was on top of my mom, slamming his body violently between her legs. Aside from not understanding what I was seeing, I was also trying to figure out why there was a gun in his hand, aimed at her temple. My mother's face was swollen and her dress torn. The plum from her lips was smeared across her face and chin. I wanted to say something, but I didn't. My father had to have known I came in the room, but he did not stop his thrusting. When my mother's eyes set on me, I backed away and closed the door softly as though I had never entered. I cried in a corner until he came out and simply said, "Let's go. I don't want to get caught in that five o'clock traffic."

That was one of many life-altering incidents. My father's reputation in the neighborhood was no longer a good one. Our home became decorated with chaos, cursing, and war wounds from my father's fists. Over time, I watched my mother transform from a feisty warrior to a skittish weakling. The waves of my father's physical and verbal abuse eroded any fight my mother possessed. She didn't even bat an eye when he doused the house in gasoline and threatened to light it with us inside. For the life of me I didn't understand why he kept coming around if he wanted nothing to do with us. Again, being young, I did not yet understand that I was watching a sociopath. According to the neighbors, my father was always hanging around the house and it didn't help that he had turned into an alcoholic. Because the threats began to come more frequently, being placed in state custody became the protective order of choice by the judge.

When we arrived at the home of the Peterson family, I could see that they were nice and it was a comfortable home, but something within me couldn't warm up to them. My two siblings and I sat at their table. Mrs. Peterson looked like a Stepford wife as she served us food that was nothing close to what we were used to. She spoke of me as if I wasn't there and told Mr. Peterson that I must not be eating because I was traumatized.

I didn't know what that meant then, but now that I know, honestly, the only thing traumatizing me in that moment was that meal with no seasoning whatsoever. It was like licking cardboard. Yuck! It is unfortunate that my focus then wasn't on the sanctuary that the Peterson home offered, only that they were different from us, beginning with their skin color, and Mrs. Peterson was not my Mama. So, I was overly happy to return home.

I assume that the courts came to some agreement with my mom and dad, because my dad was allowed visitation rights, but things never really changed. The new reoccurrence of this codependent non-relationship was my mom fussing because my dad would promise to pick us up, but never show. Sometimes I have flashes of memories where I am sitting at the window all night waiting for my dad and he is a no-show. I always convinced myself that he was only late, stuck in the traffic that he complained about so often.

The times that he would show up there was the new dynamic of having to deal with the girlfriends and/or baby-mamas that he collected over the years. By now I was in that pre-pubescent age bracket, and I began to hate going with my dad for visits because he always wanted us to fit into his world instead of him being a father and becoming a part of ours.

When the divorce was officially finalized, family stories suggest that my mom had a nervous breakdown. All the signs had been there but, if it can be called lucky, we missed most of it since she was at least aware enough to hire babysitters. Once she became more stable, she found her independence as an LPN, a licensed practical nurse.

Her studies and dedication to having a profession paid off, but we had become latchkey children. When you are the oldest in such a situation, it is you who becomes the parent. As young as I still was, I was now responsible for myself and siblings. As good as I had become at that, we still had other issues to deal with. Food was hard to come by and it was more than difficult for a hungry child to tell other hungry children to tough it out. At times, my mother saw fit to send us into the care of others so our basic needs could be met, but we would be split up.

My brother went to his godparents, my sister went to her godmother, and I went to my aunt's or the neighbors' house. I am not too sure what my sister's and brother's feelings were about being separated, but I hated going to my aunt's and I hated being babysat by the neighbors. The neighbors had 12 children and the house was so chaotic that no one paid attention when anyone was out of place. Their son Terry always managed to make sure that he and I were out of place together.

He was in his early teens and nothing but hormones. I didn't know this phase of life for young people until the day he told me he had a fun game for us to play, just me and him, away from all of the noise. I followed him down the creaky stairs into the musky basement. It was cluttered with holiday decorations with a silence I could celebrate. I took a deep breathe in, to soak up the quiet that was missing from my life for so long. I appreciated the stillness, I could hear the oxygen entering my body on my inhale. I remembered why we were in the basement, and wondered why we would disturb such peace..

"What are we going to play, Terry?" I asked. "Where are the board games at? I don't see any here." He unbuckled his belt and removed it from his trousers. "What are you doing?"

Terry unbuttoned and unzipped his pants. He pulled them and his underwear down to his thighs, revealing his erect penis. I stood frozen, having flashbacks of my dad when he had raped my mother. Terry took the belt, formed a loop and yanked both sides, causing it to make a loud snapping noise as the two strips of leather slapped together. I jumped out of the memory of my parents into the reality of Terry.

"Touch it," he said firmly.

I didn't move, and he threatened to whip me if I didn't do it. He snapped the belt again and my trembling hand reached for him. He smiled and moaned a little.

"That's it. Now stroke it," he commanded.

I didn't understand what he meant by that so he hit me, before showing me with his own hand what he wanted me to do. I pulled on it the way he showed me and he kept making noises. At some point he said I should kiss it. When I didn't do it immediately, he grabbed my hair hard and again told me to kiss it. I leaned forward and kissed it, continuing to pull on it.

There was something clear and sticky coming from it, followed by sprays of white that hit me in the face. I started to cry and he threw a towel at me, telling me to clean myself up. He warned that I better not tell anyone. I don't know what I thought would happen, but I knew what a threatening tone was. It became the norm when I had to go to the neighbors.

    I would like to be able to say that it was better at my aunt's place, but it wasn't. My uncle was drunk all the time, my aunt constantly spoke negative words about my life, and my drug-abusing cousin had an extremely violent temper. I suppose the drug abuse was to dull the pain of his parents' lifestyle, as well as helping him coming to terms with his admission of being homosexual in a less tolerant time. Once I saw my cousin outside of the house with what I now know was his boyfriend. My cousin was doing the same thing to the man that Terry had asked me to do. I thought he too was being forced and I wanted to help him. I picked up a clock and opened the window, thinking I would throw it at the man, but then I became very confused. My cousin stood up and kissed the man, and they said "I love you" to each other.

    "I need to have you inside me," the man said. "Not here. My mom and pops might see." "Then let them see," he replied.

He kissed my cousin again. They went slightly more into the shadows but I could still see them. The man made his body more accessible to my cousin and he entered him, repeatedly thrusting. Again, I had had disturbing memory flashes of my parents and Terry. I slammed the window shut and the two of them scuffled around in surprise. Moments later, my cousin was in the room with me. He had me pinned against the wall by the throat. I could barely breathe, but could nod just enough to agree to keep my mouth shut about what I saw.

That was the light side of the violence at my aunt's place. Every other day, fights broke out among them, including drawing knives on each other. On occasion, people did get cut. Somehow, in all the craziness, I did have fun at times with my other cousins there that were my age, but it never failed to be interrupted. We would be listening to music or watching a show and there she would be.

"What are your lazy asses doing in here? I thought I told you get those dishes done and take out the trash!" my aunt would yell shrilly.

"Auntie, we were just…"

An extension cord, the thick brown kind, whipped through the air with a cracking noise to eat into my side.

My agonizing scream did nothing to stop her as she hit me repeatedly in different spots, until she run out of labored insults and was truly out of breath. My rising welts and torn skin brought no tenderness from her.

"Now get your little ass in that kitchen and clean up!"

I could never figure out why my aunt was so mean or said such demeaning things to me. As time went on, she switched to beating me with a long white extension cord, the kind often used as ropes for double-dutch. The stinging red welts on my back, legs and arms left bruises and scarring that I learned to hide well. Just like with my cousin, just like with Terry, I remained silent and pretended that there was nothing but joy in my life. It is amazing to me that something so simple as growing older created a change for me. The visits to other homes soon came to an end because I was legally old enough to stay home alone for extended periods of time.

Being at home more often, I discovered that my mom was behind in her bills. Since she had no one else to help her, I felt the full force of that burden. My mom came up to my school and requested a work permit for me. There I was at the age of 14, working at Burger King, and further perfecting my mask of happiness. I was taking on the responsibility of helping my mom with monthly bills and childhood was surely a thing of the past.

This went on for about six months until she met Kenneth, the man who soon would become our new father figure. Life became a lot better. He was definitely a provider, but there was one problem: Kenneth was married. Mom continued to see him on the grounds that he was separated from his wife. He was a good man and he definitely made my mom smile. He gave our family hope. We no longer had to struggle—no more days of sitting in the house without electricity, eating sugar bread sandwiches and government cheese. We had finally got our childhood back and did family activities such as vacations and amusement parks. One good quality that my mom had is she never missed a birthday: she always acknowledged me and my siblings on our birthdays. She would go overboard with the parties she gave us in observance of our birthdays. I appreciated my mom for always acknowledging my special day. However, I really could have done without the parties, if I could have traded them for her quality time, love and ear.

Even though all that Kenneth did was good, I still felt empty because my mom began to consume all her time with Kenneth and my younger siblings. I began to feel like the black sheep of the family. She was there for me, just not in the ways I needed her. I needed my mom to listen to me and converse with me. I guess she just didn't know how to do that.

I had reached a place of having no respect for my mother. I wanted to hurt her like she had hurt me with her repeated abandonment. We constantly got into arguments and physical fights. I wonder now if it is because when she looked at me, she saw my father. If she couldn't stand the sight of him, how could she stomach seeing his strong genes in me? There came a time when it was clear that my mom had finally got tired of fighting with me, because every other day she would call the police or juvenile authorities to come pick me up.

My father had only gotten away with as much torment as he laid on us because he was protected by an unspoken code among officers. The same is transferrable to an officer's children. Go figure. This was the only time I had some real quality time with my father. When I would arrive to the juvenile facility, I would just wait to be picked up by my dad and I was never really booked into the facility. What was my mom thinking when she called the police on me? It only made me angrier, and confirmed what I already had in my mind—that she didn't want me. Outside of her repeatedly telling me that, of course… So I became a runaway, trying to escape from her since she treated me like an outcast.

The streets were dark in all senses of the word. I don't know what I was thinking.

On many nights I wondered why I didn't just keep up with my work at Burger King, secretly save money, and take myself away to something good, rather than what I ran to. I started doing things beyond my character in order to survive. The worst place I ever ended up was in a crack house. A friend I had made in the streets told me everything would be fine and she slept there often without trouble. It didn't take long for trouble to find me there, though. In the back of the house was a large man who sat in a busted leather chair like a king. He had a harem of gaunt-faced women in dirty underwear lying at his feet like cats. When he first saw me, he stood and, with a sheepish smile, asked me to come to him. He told me that I looked hungry and asked if I wanted to have something to eat.

Taking a handful of cash from his pocket, he said, "I can give you anything you want, baby girl. Help me and I will definitely help you."

He licked his lips with a sway and I felt

uncomfortable. I stammered in nervousness as I declined. I backed up and his face quickly went from offense to anger. He drew a gun and told me not to take another step. He ordered the half-alert women to leave the room. They obeyed, floating off like the ghosts they were. However, one stopped.

She whispered listlessly, "No worries, child. It will only hurt for a little bit."

Before I could take another breath or process what was happening to me, he grabbed me. I tried to fight back, but he knocked me down with such force that it made my aunt's beatings seem like a kiss on the forehead. I felt his hand slide into my pants.

"Just the way I like it. Nice and tight," he said.

He groped me and planted his chapped lips all over me. I wanted to be somewhere else… anywhere else. *Welcome to Burger King, may I take your order?* I couldn't disappear, though. The reality of what was happening was not going to be replaced by such wishes. He licked on me and screamed at me, demanding to know why I wasn't getting wet. I didn't understand what he meant by it. I just begged him to stop. He told me to shut up and placed the gun at my head. There I was with him between my legs, thrusting into me like my dad did to my mom. I imagined I looked just like her, on my back and accepting the pain of what was happening. I looked out to see my friend standing there looking at us and, just like I had, she left trying to pretend she hadn't walked in on anything.

When it was all done, he yelled at me to get out. I told him he tore my clothes and he shot a bullet near my feet. I ran out half-clothed, ending up in a park close to home. Then I passed out. By some strange miracle, when I woke up screaming and fighting, it was at home, in the arms of my mother, who was trying to wipe my face with a warm cloth. Though I was relieved when I realized this, I refused to show it. I got up and shut myself off in the bathroom. I stayed in there for hours after she stopped banging on the door and telling me that I had to go to the doctor because she could tell what had happened to me this time; exactly what she had always warned me about.

She never knew it, but the only thing that gave me hope when I ran away from home was that my mom would at least look for me. This gave me some assurance that she halfway cared. Still, if I could have had it my way, I would have ended up with my grandmother. She became the mother figure of my mind and, though I didn't always have access to her in the early years, I feel that for the most part she always was the one who understood what it was to love a child fully. That trouble, like all trouble, passed; however, it soured the energy of our home even more.

In all the chaos that was my family, eventually Kenneth, the only thing that was good in our lives, left. I am not certain of all the details of the breakup but, from then on, I watched my mom go in and out of relationships as she looked for love. But I never understood why all the men she dated were married or about to get a divorce (so she said).

It's as if she was knowingly or unknowingly trying to become what she believed destroyed her... the other woman. It was a peculiar style of vengeance. My mom needed love so desperately that her priorities were all out of whack. She always put her boyfriends before her children's needs. Again, this made me mad watching her cater to those men and not me and my siblings. As time went on, I grew older and got past my pain enough to date.

My first attempt at dating didn't go as well as I had hoped. This could well have been because his name was Terry and I had too many memories of the neighbor and the things he made me do. Later in my teen life came Joe, whom my mother and I met at a job referral program we visited. He was seven years older than me, yet my mom consented to his request to date me. I was pleased by his audacity to approach my mother for permission to date me. Joe was handsome and very generous with overflow of income. There wasn't a thing I asked for that he didn't buy.

As he was a lot older than me, he wanted do things that I just simply was not ready for because I had shut down that part of myself. I still wasn't even sure if I was over the bad feeling I had had for my first boyfriend. Joe was always frustrated by me not having sex with him but never pushed, likely because of the legalities he knew existed. On my 18th birthday, my mother and I had an argument because, for the first time ever, she didn't celebrate my special day. The fight was so huge that it became physical. When I saw her grab the phone after I scratched her face, I thought she was calling the police, which by now never fazed me.

How shocked I was when I heard my mom say, "Joe, come pick this little bitch up before I kill her…"

I'm not too sure why she opted not to call my dad at least, but this night was the night my life changed forever. I cried and begged my mom to let me stay. I didn't want to go with him. My pleas fell on deaf ears. She put as much of my stuff as she could grab into a black plastic 30-gallon trash bag.

"I'll show you," she said, shoving the bag into my chest and pushing me out the door. "You have always been a selfish little bitch who only thinks of yourself and that is all you will ever be. I hate you. I'm done raising your ungrateful ass."

"But Mom?"

"You lost your right to call me mom. You are not my daughter anymore," she said, pointing at the wound on her face. "Leave me to raise my real children."

Joe pulled up and tears just rolled from my eyes. We hadn't been long at his house when he kissed me. I was just frozen as he explored my body. I envisioned everyone who had ever taken advantage of me sexually and again had visions of my dad forcing my mom. I told him that I didn't want to have sex and that I was practically still a virgin. He scoffed at me, telling me that my mom had told him all about me.

Joe said, "You can't live anywhere for free. Tonight you're going to become a real woman."

When he moved from my vagina to my rectum, I saw images of my cousin giving anal sex to his boyfriend. It was so painful to me, yet my cousin's boyfriend had seemed to be enjoying it. I was so glad when he was done. In the fetal position, I lay on the bloodied sheets for hours as Joe snored next to me.

When he woke, he forced me to give him oral sex and punched me in the head if my teeth grazed him wrong. As I gagged and sucked him, learning what I didn't want to learn, a deeper hate for my mother developed. I felt that, if I saw her pass me on the street, I would murder her.

In a strange turn of events, I saw my stepsister at a market one day. I told her the truth about where I was and what Joe was like. Before I knew it, she had made sure that I went to go live with my dad, because it was evident to her that my mom and I would never be able to stay under the same roof again. Her behavior had created such opinions in me that keeping silent was no longer a part of my spirit. When I told my dad with my own words what had happened, he relished the idea that she was an awful mom and took pleasure in joining me in tearing her down.

I thought living with my dad would be better, but the grass was not greener. I guess perception is everything. How can anyone process all this mental anguish while dealing with parents too caught up in their own problems to tend to their children? Neither of them was capable of listening to or understanding me. I could tell that to my mom I was a little bitch and to my dad I was stupid. He gave me that label when it thought it made sense for me to busy my time by earning some money. Listening to him, I went back to what I knew. I returned to working in fast food and I even made a friend named Mariah. She was very pretty. She was Hawaiian and black with extremely long hair. I took to her since she was older than me and it seemed that she looked out for me… but the friendship was not perfect. She taught me how to steal from the register but when it came up short more than once, I got fired. Not taking me for a thief, the manager figured I lacked good calculation skills.

    Mariah and I remained friends after I got fired. The closer we became, the more secrets she shared. One big one was that she went both ways. I don't know why, but I let her kiss me and when she undressed in front of me, I actually got excited. The things we did together gave me fever to even think about and I was okay with what we were becoming—until she tried to introduce me to something else. Mariah smoked crack cocaine. I learned this when I had her over at my dad's house and we had just got through pleasuring each other. She sat there smashing a Coke can, placing the rocks where she had smashed it, lighting the can from the opening that you drink out of and pretty much freebasing. The smell was awful. She wanted me to join her, but I refused.

Instead, as hard as it was, I kicked her out. My dad interrogated me about the odor because, in his line of work, it was familiar, but he believed me when I assured him I didn't know. I said that I thought our Asian neighbors were cooking something strange again.

    I barely had time to think of Mariah, but I saw her from time to time. It was hard watching her go on binges, knowing the things she had to do to get drugs when she had no money. I tried to convince her to go to rehab, but we ended up wrestling right in the middle of the street. I didn't want to really hurt her, so I stopped while I was ahead and told her again to get some help.

    My dad worked a lot, so he was oblivious to most of my life. He was almost never home and the days he was there he would have some tramp over. I resented all of them, especially when they had the nerve to tell me to clean the house and kitchen after they had messed it up. Back then, it didn't seem to me that it was simply a matter of chores and helping out because I lived there rent-free. Instead, it felt like Cinderella on her most awful days before a prince was even close to being in the picture. I decided that if they didn't care, I didn't either. Life became a big party. I began to run the house like it was mine. Despite my feelings about certain things and experiences, I started dating drug dealers right up under my dad's nose. I was looking for love in all the wrong places.

I was looking for love in all the wrong places. I was just fixated on doing the wrong things anything to undercut my parents authority and to make them both hurt like they had hurt me! I befriended a young lady by the name of Deon that I had met in the past our paths had crossed again. She was from the rough side of town where I would often hang out. Deon's cognitive state was slow, but she was cool. She was someone that truly had my back, understood loyalty and always looked out for me I had practically moved my new best friend and her children into the house. I guess this was my way of spiting my father who was never home and paying her back in some type of way.

The only regret I had in all of it was Demetrius. I originally met him during my runaway time. He too was a drug dealer small time runner not top shelf like I usually would date and we strayed from pillar to post. This guy ended up getting high off his own supply… the thing that you *never* do if you are in the game. One day, when he needed a fix, he stole everything I owned, including my car, to barter for drugs. Being someone who still hung with the same crowd, I received a phone call from a friend who said she had seen my car circling a particular neighborhood. In a heartbeat, my demand for a car and gun was met. I left all those people behind partying in my dad's house. I drove straight to the neighborhood and while in route, I actually saw my car traveling along. I pulled in front of my car, blowing the horn, first short beeps and then a long drawn-out one. The guy screeched the car to a halt and got out with his gun.

"That's my car!" I screamed, getting out and drawing my gun as well. We argued back and forth in the middle of the street. I don't know what possessed him to bargain with me, but he did.

"Look, I don't have time for this shit. I am just a runner, I don't make any decisions. If you want your car back, you have to follow me back to the house," he said.

I followed him back to a house, where I had to speak to someone who I guess was the head guy. It was a very dangerous situation and I could have been killed, but I got that car back. The runner actually drove it home for me. It was surreal and something that you would never think would really happen. I would also later find out it was only because I was recognized as a cop's kid by someone doing an undercover sting on the whole operation. I got back to my dad's place at the same time as he was bursting in on the party and kicking everyone out.

We had a major blowout then.

"Oh, now you want to be a father and regulate with rules? It's too late for that."

My father slapped me hard. My face was swollen for days, but I didn't back down. We argued all the time. I wanted his love, attention, and acceptance so bad that it was worth it to me to argue with him. My dad gave me more than a little bit of hell, though. I admit that thinking I could go toe-to-toe with a police officer, a trained killer, was illogical, but anger makes people do thoughtless things.

Finally, I just said to myself, *Forget it*. I played nice. I did chores. I cooked meals. I smiled and played the role of the perfect daughter in order to gain his trust. Just when he thought I had really changed, I tried to poison him. I made the mistake of inviting guests over. I wanted others whom he hurt in life to see him die too. My stepsister arrived while I was still cooking and kept asking to help. Maybe I said one too many ominous things, but she observed me so close that she caught me stirring boric acid into the mashed potatoes.

"I knew something was up. You are trying to kill us!" she yelled, knocking the potato bowl to the floor.

She was in hysterics and I grabbed her, trying to calm her. "No, sweetie, it's not for you. It's not for any of you. It's for him. He betrayed all of us."

"Get your hands off of me! You have lost your mind," my sister cried out, shoving me away.

She fled faster than I ever saw her move before. She called her mom and her mom called my dad to tell him. So I had to go to Plan B. When he arrived to confront me, I was ready. The night before, I had sneaked one of my then-boyfriend's guns out of his apartment. I slipped it right into my purse and he was none the wiser, because he was high and in a lull from our sex anyway.

My father came in ready to fight.

"Where are you, crazy bitch?"

I came out of the bedroom shooting, but I missed. My father ran and I chased him. When he ran past my car, I hopped in and started to chase him in my car. It seemed I was becoming quite good at this method of intimidation. I was on his heels. If I wanted to crush him under the vehicle I could have, but I was far more entertained by seeing him run. I drove ahead of him and then slammed on the brakes, causing him to run into the car and suffer some minor injuries. I got out of the car and held the gun to his forehead as he lay on his back in pain. I had made up my mind that he was going to listen to what I had to say. Talk about crazy! From me poured all the horrors that I had gone through since the day he left my family. I thought that after all of that drama my dad was going to put me out of his house, but he didn't; at least not that night. However, he was furious!

I woke the next day to a refrigerator that had been chained and locked cutting off all access to the food that was in it. Locks had been installed on the food pantry doors and the electricity had been cutoff to my bedroom. This trough me into a further fit of rage! I drove to my father's job and asked what the hell was wrong with him! His reply was he does not take care of grown folks yet alone someone who tried to kill him.

I guess I get that shoot-it-up cowboy mentality from him. It was no different than the time when he held my grandmother (his mom) hostage one night. I made sure to remind him of how crazy he had been then, repeatedly turned the gun to his own head and ours. Talk about dysfunctional! But he always had a reason for everything. At that time, my dad blamed his mother because his girlfriend, who he loved and wanted to marry, dumped him after she found out he had cheated on her. I really didn't understand then why he blamed his mother, but he thought the solution to his heartache would be to kill her, me, and him. I later discovered that my grandmother, tired of being asked where her son was all the time, intentionally sent his girlfriend to an address where she would see for herself that she wasn't the only one. I was just there in the wrong place at the wrong time under her care, but it mattered little to him whether I was there or not, as always.

Looking back, the entire hostage incident was really sad because my grandmother had Parkinson's disease and I remember her shaking from that rather than fear. It was a quick head tremble that was slight, but noticeable nonetheless. It was a constant nod that stood out as she tried to convince my dad to put the gun down. After 30 minutes of this drama I guess I was just tired and thought he was nuts. I had actually accepted that I would die at the hands of my father and that would be my story.

At that point I already felt I had nothing to live for and I didn't care if he pulled the trigger. I was more concerned about my grandmother so made a bold move out the front door. I heard the gun click but it didn't fire. Part of me felt like it was a sham. Surely if he was going to do something he would have done it already. So I looked at him and said plainly, "You are crazy," and left out the front door. Even though I was scared and I took my chances by leaving, I pushed my luck a little further and called for help since my grandmother was still in the house. His police friends intervened and that was that, all swept under the rug.

The commonality with all my family members appeared to be that we all wanted to be loved, but didn't have common sense enough to love and value each other. After those many nights of arguments with my dad and the big blowup, I thought we finally had an understanding.

Unfortunately, it didn't take long before it all got physical again. I remember him being upset because I didn't do the dishes, but I think it was more than that. He had been looking for a reason, a good trigger, so he could get back at me. He yelled as usual and I started washing dishes, clanging them without breaking them. As he continued to fuss, I did not notice that he had slipped on his driving gloves. He stood on his coffee table and slowly untwisted the hot bulb of the overhead light. He threw it and it hit the floor near me, the heated fragments of the bulb hitting my skin.

I got so mad I said to myself, *Tonight is the night I am going to fight him, gun or no gun.* I cussed him out so bad he slapped me, but I was so fueled by hatred that I felt nothing and stood strong. I barely took a step back before I struck him in the face. A tussle started and my breathing was labored from broken ribs by the time I called the police. Would you believe I ended up being the one arrested? The boys in blue really do stick together.

I apparently had enough unpaid fines to do some time and neither of my parents came for me. Eventually I was released on my own recognizance and I had nowhere to go when released. I couldn't go to my mom's because she was in a new relationship. I remember calling her, asking if I could come, but she told me that she and her family was at peace and she wasn't going to allow me to disrespect her family. As if I wasn't family.

This was coming from a woman who was verbally abusive and, though not as bad as my aunt, sometimes physically abusive. She was always accusing me of selling drugs and sex because of the people I dated and hung out with. I sold nothing, even if they all did. Most of my young life she threatened to put me in a girls' home. I was hurt by the things she said because in her suffering, she did not acknowledge mine. It was as though she saw my life only in those moments captured on the home videos, the fake moments where we were actors in our own tragedy.

Maybe it was her coping mechanism to only imagine that our lives went untouched by her drama but even in that consideration, I still don't understand her. At any rate, I spent one night at a friend's house. I will never forget that night. I love my friend, but her house was mice-infested. I remember just sitting in a chair all night with my feet propped up, trying to sleep and block out the sound of the mice moving about. I left her house and spent a couple nights in a trap house—the place where drug dealers keep cash and product. After this aimless wandering, I bottled up my pride and most prodigally went to my grandmother. She took me in and I really appreciated it, because she stood by me no matter what.

I stayed with my grandmother for about a year. I eventually met a guy named Paul who was an older, distinguished man. I liked Paul a lot because he taught me how to grow intellectually and as a person. Although I still had quite a few anger issues stemming from my past, Paul taught me how to be a lady as he treated me as such, challenging me to go after the finer things in life.

I really appreciated Paul for trying to help me find resolve through counseling; however, I am not too sure if counseling actually helped. Sure, it provided a pathway for me to vent and talk about situations that were bothering me. Nevertheless, I still stayed angry. I believe the only good thing that came from counseling was that I learned how to confront my issues. I did what the counselor suggested, which was to tell both my parents, without anger or weapons, how they hurt me and how I felt.

Oddly enough, my dad was more receptive to this discussion than my mother. My dad actually apologized and became more attentive to my feelings and that's all I really ever wanted from my parents. That was the first step to me and my father forming a better relationship. As for my mom, she still doesn't think she did anything wrong. There is still much work to be done with my relationship with her, but counseling didn't teach me how to leave the hurt and pain behind. The struggle with hurt and pain is a daily uphill battle, but there is more to come on that and the magic of Paul… Paul who had me remembering the fashionista in me and knowing when I looked in the mirror that I was beautiful.

I may as well have been Keri Hilson singing out, "My walk, my talk, the way I dress, it's not my fault so please don't trip. Don't hate me cause I'm beautiful!" That Pretty Girl Rock side of me wasn't new, though. It was just resurrected, so to speak, and it was a good thing. Just because my family went through things didn't mean we weren't on the top of our game. Like most people in an elaborate coverup, we knew that looking good was key to the trickery. My entire family dresses their asses off.

My siblings and I were taught at a very young age, *Never look like you feel and always dress for success*. And now that I am adult I just call it, *Winning Through Intimidation*, thanks to Robert J. Ringer. Honestly, 'fashionista' is not a word that I usually use to describe myself. Yes, I dress my best Monday to Friday while working or conducting business (yes, business… the good part is coming); however, catch me on the weekend and you will find me most often in sweats or workout clothes with a ball cap on.

I haven't mentioned school much, because it was as much as a disaster as my home life. I was the awkward kid who was picked on during elementary school, and it was hard for me to make friends because every few months or so I was changing schools due to how my mother dealt with her personal situations. Many along the way started calling me bourgeois, because I became more introverted but had on all the right brands that would get me into the top cliques at school. That type of vanity was never me. I was quite the opposite. I am very sensitive, caring, and always ready to serve individuals that need my help.

I just consider Paul as being a springboard for my realization that I needed to embrace the principle behind self-care. As I've navigated through my adult life, I've become proud of having my own style and the presentation my parents embedded in me. If I could have gained anything good from them, let it be something that simple… How you dress affects your entire mental capacity. And, given all I have been through, I will continue to be radical, sassy, and classy. So my statement to men that make this comment is, *No, honey, not bourgeois… Just too much woman for you.* And for the females that claim the same, *I have no control over the insecurities that exist within you.* As you will soon find out, I have had enough of my own to deal with.

Chapter Two
Realized

In the past, I was clearly unhappy personally, professionally, and emotionally because of my traumatic experiences. I often asked why nothing was going right in my life. What would it take to get it to go right? Why couldn't I find happiness? What did I do to deserve a life of continuing struggle? I finally realized that I hadn't done anything wrong and that life itself is an ongoing process. It is up to the individual to view life as negative or positive.

Earlier on, I sometimes felt as if I wasn't good enough for the people in my life. I'm not the same person I was then. It would be frightening if I were. Although the essential feeling is still very much present, my life has changed enormously and some of the experiences I have had have altered the way I see myself and the world around me. It's called growth.

In the later part of the year 2002 I reassessed my life following a long, intense, and accidental intimate relationship with Paul. (The word accidental is used **only** because there is a huge age difference between myself and the love of my life.) Although the relationship ended badly, it was the source of an awakening that shook up my life. I was devastated. I was also grateful. It was the turning point. I realized God was trying to get my attention. Although Paul was not the right man for me, as I mentioned, his presence in my life, my heart, and my bed made it possible for me to see myself as a woman capable of both giving and receiving love.

I was determined to reinvent my life so that the loving and loved vibes would be with me always. I was determined to open up that part of me that I had hidden even from myself. The biggest change in my life these past 12 months is that I have gradually come to understand what it is to be loved just the way I am. I don't think there was ever a point in my childhood that who I was wasn't being compared to who someone else wanted me to be. On some level, I guess I understand that. The pressures on women in society to be beautiful ultimately lead to women's low self-esteem. When I was in elementary school, I was gawky and skinny.

Therefore, I was picked on a lot and my self-esteem was low. By my early twenties I began to blossom in looks and self-confidence, but I was wild enough to waste it on more trouble.

I was in and out of jail for fighting. It didn't take much to set me off. One time I was standing in line at a U.S. Post Office. A man bumped into me on his way to the section with all the boxes and tape for sale. He did not apologize. I couldn't shake off the anger that was in me for the disrespect. I stomped over to him and tapped him on the shoulder. He turned around with a look of confusion on his face.

"You are supposed to say excuse me, motherfucker!"

He didn't even have a chance to respond before I used an open-hand chop to his temple. I failed to do it the way my dad once taught me, to knock him out, but I could see his delirium and that his ears were possibly ringing. I did not know he was not alone and his daughter, around my size, came and jumped on my back. She stabbed me in my side with a nail file and it stabbed me pretty good. For the first time in a long time I was bleeding quite terribly. Oh, she had done it then. I flipped her off of me onto the floor. I got on top of her and pummeled her face until her dad pulled me off. Who knows what he intended to do next, but the cops were already there arresting me.

This time it was more complicated than other times, because it was on federal property. Federal property means federal time. With the charges of Simple Assault and Aggravated Assault I had no clue what to expect. As I bided my time in jail, I didn't know what to do between the multiple court cases. One day an elderly inmate with a kind face passed me a bible. I couldn't help but wonder how such a sweet woman ended up in there. Along the way we talked and I found out she had killed her husband for sexually abusing her daughter from another relationship. Initially I celebrated this because that is what I thought any real mom would do, but then she told me her regrets and how her daughter had been passed from foster home to foster home, where she continued to be abused because she did not think with a level head. It gave me food for thought—as she intended.

During this time of waiting for my fate to be handed to me, I was lucky that I was able to reach out from inside myself to seek God and a positive future, and realize that I had many outstanding qualities to offer. I was overcome with emotion on the day that I was told that the case had been thrown out of court due to self-defense and the record had been sealed. As I continued to try and find myself beyond the things that hurt me, I found it challenging but not unachievable. I had spent the majority of my life being compared to the sister who was easy to get along with and the brother who never did anything wrong. I spent eight years with Paul, a man who wanted to do things his way and not see me for the woman I had become. I spent all of my adult life surrounded by miscellaneous people who appreciated my intelligence or my wit. They were clueless about who I really was, but how could they know? How could I expect them to be mind-readers? Of course, I was hiding essential parts of myself all this while. I was denying my pent-up anger over life, past relationships, and other things. I was burying my need for affection behind my brains and sharp tongue, and running as fast as I could away from anyone who might possibly get through the barriers I had put up. I had to reveal myself.

Most people do think that I am a nice person but, like most people in the world, I sometimes have thoughts I am ashamed of. For example, when my brother lost his job, I was very concerned, supportive, and, I think, helpful to him. There was also a part of me that thought he had got what he deserved, that he had brought this on himself and, in a weird way, I was almost joyful about it. I decided to tell someone who would become my closest friend about these thoughts, and he was able to accept that I had those thoughts without it changing how he felt about me or him thinking that my concern for my brother was less than genuine. He understood that I could have these dark thoughts without being a bad person. Not having to hide that part of me has been a relief. This friend is God.

    I never really understood how important communication really was until God began to tear down the walls surrounding my heart. I was always a talker. I talked to win—to drown people in words and get my way. It usually worked. I went on and on about what I thought, but seldom spoke about how I felt, and I usually set the agenda. I guess this was my way of making the pain go away. Although I'm still growing, I've learned to appreciate and compensate for others' strengths and weaknesses. I've learned to cheer for others' personal success and to comfort those who do not succeed. The rough edges of my personality are being rubbed away as I settle into my new life with Christ. I am discovering the one true way, the way of Jesus Christ.

    Life is filled with ups and downs. We have our good days and bad days, some days worse than others.

Consciousness brings more pain, but it also brings more joy. As God begins to mend the broken heart you will begin to seek a positive future. If you press into God far enough, you will begin to see things you had never seen before. In addition, if you reach still further, you will begin to allow God to fulfill your ultimate destiny.

     Remember, God can't dwell in an unclean vessel. First, you must eliminate the old baggage. You may call it clichéd, but replace the negative with the positive. Identify everything that is negative in your life so that a resolution is possible. Although it takes time and effort to accomplish your desires and goals, when you are ready for change in your life you will be motivated to make a commitment to God and yourself. You will begin to apply yourself to achieving an inner healing. Just remember what is going on inside you didn't happen overnight and will not disappear overnight. Trust God; walk by Faith and not by sight. I did, and I wouldn't exchange what I feel now for anything in the world.

Chapter Three
Deliver Me

Church was introduced to me as a young child. I was involved with the choir, usher board, and holiday skits… the whole nine. However, I had my first encounter with God in November 2002. When I explain this to people, they often look at me as being a *baby* Christian; at least this has been my experience. It has often bothered me; not that it is bothersome in the sense of my being incapable of receiving direction or correction, but rather of my having to deal with the problem of older women trying to run my life. They did not understand that I was not a baby trying to learn how to walk, but a woman who had lived life in a way that reached me far beyond my years in life lessons and application of wisdom gained.

Rather than a baby Christian, I was a *gravida* who needed nourishment for what she held within. I needed frequent visits to the Supreme Doctor to ensure proper development. As a gravida, in order to ensure total wellness during the gestational period, it is very important to know what type of exercises you can do, what type of diet to eat and things to be avoided. My wellness was delayed, unfortunately, because the well-meaning elders clouded my mind with muddled messages laced with condemnation and instillation of fear that drew me further and further away from where I was originally headed. I was stuck in this loop of drama constantly going round and round. The people coming in and out of my life were different, but the spirit each person carried was the same: manipulation, gossip and deception. What a revelation it was, to say the least. It had been a dark spiritual day when what I had been blind to became apparent. I was certain that, even if they were fellow Christians, I had to remove certain people from my life.

    Three in particular, the closest to me, had to go first: Donna, Anna, and Kathy. Collectively, we were the opposite of what we should have been. It dawned on me when I passed a store window, seeing my weary guilt-ridden reflection while also observing a display of monkey statues emulating *see no evil, speak no evil, hear no evil, and do no evil*. That wisdom was surely missed with us. I also would come to learn that when I didn't move people on my own, they would be removed without my consent if that is what the Supreme Doctor had prescribed. I would take my medicine and like it.

It started with Donna. She was someone I considered my ace and will always hold a spot close to my heart. There is no doubt in my mind that she loves God and that she always had my best interest at hand; however, she was a drama queen. There was never a dull moment and she always thought a person had a hidden agenda; consequently this kept us at each other's throats. Our relationship ended when I realized she resurrected in me the former self that would fight or consider permanently ending a life, like I had attempted with my father. I did not want to be that person. The feeling came to me in church, of all places. Donna prided herself in her work as the treasurer but she also often seemed overwhelmed. Knowing this, I went to the pastor and suggested that I could assist her, since I had a background in cash handling through my work. The pastor thought it was a good idea.

After he told her about my offer, she smiled and told him sweetly that I could start helping the following week. She thanked me in front of him, but what happened after this floored me. As I helped her, she would start constant arguments with me when I noted oversights and miscalculations. She would rant about all her banking experience and how she was an MBA, while also belittling me and what I had to offer. She questioned my motive in volunteering all the time and would comment that people from the streets often get tempted when around large amounts of money. She suggested that I help somewhere else, where I would be less prone to break a commandment.

By then, I knew something was up with Donna. I felt betrayed and in my observance, I knew I had placed heat on her. Having learned what I learned from Mariah, I picked up on what Donna was doing. She was removing money from the tithes. It wasn't small stuff like what Mariah and I had been doing back in the burger chain. It was thousands of dollars. I had no intention of ratting Donna out, but I did approach her about it right after I stepped down as her assistant.

"Donna, you're going to get caught if you keep doing this," I told her as I stood at the door of the finance room. She met me with silence and I continued, "Can you at least tell me why? What is it that you need? Maybe we can just ask for help."

"Listen, you little bitch," Donna retorted, "you keep your mouth shut or I promise you that I will make you regret the day you were ever born."

My face grew hot with rage. She sounded like my mother and I wanted to rip her tongue straight from her mouth.

"So, is that it now? That's how you treat your friends?" I asked through angered breaths.

Donna clarified, "You really are stupid, aren't you?"

There it was again… my mother's words thrown at me once more. My fist clenched.

"We never were friends," she said. "You were nothing more than an assignment, a church newbie. We are all assigned somebody. It's about retaining membership." She nodded toward the money.

I was appalled. I saw the devil in her. My nails dug into my palms. I wanted to hit her so bad, but I just couldn't. It was almost as if something was weighting my arms down and not allowing it. Staring at my fists she said, "I will no longer be sitting with you in church."

I turned and left. We didn't talk for a long time. People gossiped about our newfound distance but I got over it. I still had Anna and Kathy, right? I would see Donna watching me laugh and talk with them. It seemed to bother her and, much like an old boyfriend, I would lock eyes with her for just a moment before we averted them simultaneously. We came back to what I thought was resurrected friendship while agreeing on the deliciousness of a dish made at our monthly potluck.

She whispered to me, "I have been praying and I forgive you. God is taking me to another level. Let's chat later."

I didn't know what to think about that. Something felt wrong about it, but I ignored the feeling. I talked to her on the phone and we agreed to let our previous exchange go. I asked her if she had stopped taking money from the tithes but the call disconnected before she could answer. She called me back the next day, apologizing for her cordless phone having lost its charge and I didn't even think to ask the question again. I was feeling somewhat excited about having her back. Despite what I knew, there was something else about her that I loved and missed. Believe it or not, Donna praised and worshipped in a way I had never seen.

During church she was always all energy and fire. I believe Donna's purpose in being in my life was to show me how to openly praise God. Before our divide, I often leaned on Donna's anointing to jumpstart my praise. Imagine my surprise when I discovered that Donna still wouldn't sit next to me in church and it was because of what she had said about her new level. For some reason she felt that she had gone to a higher level in God and had to sit close to the ministry staff. So I still didn't have Donna to help start my praise, but I would also come to know that this was God's plan all along because it forced me to get into the presence of God all the more.

Donna and I continued to talk outside of church. It had become an odd relationship because it felt a bit secret. Donna began to call for favors daily and each day I became angrier at the situation. The only thing I could rehearse in my mind was that "God was taking her to another level," but she still needed me to give her rides to do errands and even attend church on Wednesdays, Sundays, and all special events in between. During some of the errands, I realized we were picking up expensive things that didn't even come close to aligning with her income. I knew in my heart how she was getting all the decorative collectors' items, jewelry, and upgraded furnishings. I was being used. Donna really began to get on my nerves with her lack of respect for our so-called friendship.

One Sunday she pushed the wrong button and I snapped—I told Donna off in front of the first lady and a group of ministers. I never mentioned the thievery aloud but blurted out many terrible things akin to every profanity I ever heard while growing up. I felt so foolish afterwards. Nevertheless, it was also a day of new beginnings. I was transitioning from being a gravida to birthing luminance. My spiritual father titled his sermon for the evening 'I'm Angry.' I was all ears and all open in heart. In his message I learned that it's okay to be angry and that God will at times shake up your world when you become comfortable. God doesn't want you focused on anything other than Him. You will get so fed up with yourself and life's events; you'll have no other choice but to stand boldly in what you are called to do. As God begins to strengthen you, he teaches you that all his children carry his anointing and no person's anointing is better than the others—it's just a matter of walking in authority. However, authority does come with a price. As God's word says, an unclean spirit goes but returns with seven spirits, more wicked than the first.

    Just when I thought I had escaped Donna's chaos, Anna and Kathy revealed their real selves. Donna's drama looked like child's play compared to the confusion they brought to my life. There was so much deception and manipulation. At times, it honestly felt like the devil had clamps on me and wouldn't let up. There was so much warfare going on in my mind. *Why am I putting up with this junk?* When I was in the world, there was so much fight in me and I didn't let anything or anyone violate me. Yet, I had managed to become Anna and Kathy's puppet.

I originally met Anna at a prayer meeting. We became close when she pulled me to the side to ask me for special prayers. I eventually learned that she wasn't working and was in the process of trying to move to California. I was in a position to help with her air travel, so I offered. Anna explained how God led her to Houston; however, she felt her time in Houston was up.

Anna stated that God had showed her a vision that her next move would be to California and that time was of the essence because she would befall tragedy if she stayed. She stated that, in her vision, every part of her life would crumble if she stayed in Houston and that, like in the destruction of Sodom, she had to leave and never look back.

Several weeks passed. Anna became very abrasive about getting to California, which threw up a red flag to me, but I never questioned her motives. Time does always tell—I later learned her trip wasn't a dying need, it was more of a want to get to a pastor whom she believed God had shown to be her future husband instead of her boyfriend at the time, who also was a member of our church but had told her he would not be interested in getting engaged any time soon.

I noted this in my memory bank and continued our acquaintance with caution and no intent on sponsoring her trip due to the way she had manipulated the truth. I should have ran as fast I could from this woman, because the signs of something not being quite right were definitely there. Ignoring this intuition generated what one could expect in not being fully attentive.

On July 4, she invited me to join her and some relatives for a drive to Galveston Beach to celebrate.

"Hon, I'm going to need you to use another name while with my family," she said. "What?" I chuckled. "Why?"

"They're nosy and I'm a private person. If they don't know who you are, they can't research you. Believe me it is better off that way. How about Janette Daniels?" she asked.

"You're serious?" I asked.

She confirmed that she was serious as a heartbeat. I wasn't buying her story and didn't agree to change my identity. Anna beat me to the punch, though. When we arrived at the hotel, she introduced me to her family as Janette. She even shared some wild story about me being an orphan from Ohio who didn't know her parents and was raised in a convent, but did not become a nun when given the option. I guess I could have busted Anna in her lie and left, but a part of me wanted to see just how far this would go. I mingled and everything appeared normal. I began to talk about God, but there was some resistance to the conversation among the group. I didn't think much of it. The night ended and we headed back to Houston.

Anna made the statement that we needed to repent for lying. By that point I had become irritated and demanded answers. Anna told me that some of her family members practice witchcraft and she didn't want them to do anything to me. She claimed she failed to tell me this before our trip because she really wanted me to go. She felt that if she told me the truth I wouldn't have wanted to go. She claimed it was to protect me, but I was furious. I couldn't understand how someone sold out for God would blindside her sister in Christ.

I did some research later and discovered that Anna was there to get their help in trying to cast a spell on me to do anything she asks of me. That taught me why it is so important to stay under God's covering. The ironic thing about all this is that four months prior I had attended a women's conference at this same hotel and one of God's prophets told me to beware of witchcraft.

Anna was being exposed for what she really was, and it was clear that she needed deliverance from the spirit of manipulation and deception if she was truly a woman of God. I began to distance myself from Anna because I refused to be back under any form of spiritual bondage.

Meanwhile there was Kathy. She was a friendly enemy and a nuisance with her cry-wolf habits. She was determined to make her issues my issues. For quite some time, I indulged and developed a sense of having to be the one to solve all of them. I gained a sense of importance because she stroked my ego with compliments of my wisdom and thanks for going above and beyond for her. The more I helped, the more drained I became.

Her needs never ceased and it was clear she was disinterested in anything that was going on with me. She was a definite *me, me, me* personality of the extreme kind. I was made fully aware of this when I was terribly sick and hospitalized. Different people had come by immediately but she only showed up a couple of days later. When she did, she didn't ask how I was feeling or what the diagnosis was. She flopped into the chair near my bed and told me all her woes, eventually asking if she could use my credit card (again) because the church pantry only offered canned goods and she wanted to buy some meats. I decided then that I couldn't allow her to infiltrate anymore.

It turned into an opportunity for me to step outside of myself, view her annoying habits, and reflect back on all the times I had dumped my problems on someone else. Looking at Kathy's behavior made me grow up and take a vow to be tactful and respectful to others' space; to bear all to God and not suck the life out of others. With Kathy, it became more of a 'distance makes the heart grow fonder' situation. I kept her in my life, but began to recognize when space was necessary for her growth and mine.

The limited experiences that I have shared of many about Donna, Anna and Kathy was not to tear them down, but to point out how easily we can slip into not recognizing how relationships with others are connected to our relationship with God as well as with ourselves. Often, God uses the negatives of relationships to reveal to us something that we also do that requires change. I can say that in each of these ladies I recognized a piece of myself that existed and I knew, based on my feelings with them, I didn't want to create that feeling in others by my presence in their lives. I wanted to bring people light, not darkness. I understand now that a person's reality is affected by their mind, will, emotions, intellect, and imaginatioin. Protect these delicate areas and don't allow them to be polluted by filth.

Chapter Four
Situations of Sex Traps and Infirmity

As one grows, certain realizations take the forefront. I observe commonalities with others.

- We are both 'Marked,' that is to say, God has stamped His finger on us
- We share the same infirmity or thorn, if you will, because we both have a high level of eroticism. Neither of us is in a position to express this passion {Rom 7:15- 20}. It is a source of confusion

Also:

- Same desire to please and be used by God

- Same love for Kingdom Business

- Same desire to see others come to know the Lord

- Same desire to receive all that God has for us

- Same humility and submission to the throne

- Same passionate lust of flesh

- Same desire to express this passion to please

- Same explicit sexual 'no boundaries' openness

- Same struggle for deliverance and complete breakthrough

- Same satanic harassment

- Same pain of cold and hot, off-and-on rollercoaster (Situation).

In this, it is obvious that, even when we know we want change, it doesn't happen overnight. The focus level often fluctuates in a way that we don't want or expect. We find ourselves in traps related to these commonalities and we either escape or stay there to rot.

Do not be victimized by negative emotions. Your flesh attempts to exploit your negative emotions in order to lead you into costly reactions.

Sex Trap

Initially it was innocent; just general conversations about God. *Situation* looked and smelled so good. I would lust intensely and wanted him so badly I would not stop until I had him. I knew what I was doing was wrong, but I had no intention of stopping. I had set my eyes on the target, was determined to hit a bullseye, and finally I did. I had managed to make myself fall for a man of God and betray his wife, family and ministry. We would have office rendezvous and it was fun. The intensity of sneaking around and knowing that other women wanted *Situation*, fueled my passion and ego. It gave me joy to know that on lunch breaks I had access to what they craved.

Situation and I would meet in the high-rise building across the street from the office in an individual restroom that was in a secluded area. We would lock the door and go for what we knew. Afterwards we'd return to our desks as if nothing happened. This unruly behavior went on for three months, and all the time I was going to church Sunday after Sunday and Wednesday after Wednesday. I would hear a message preached and conviction would come. I would say I was going to stop, but fall again. I loved God and wanted to stop, but I also loved the pleasure I was receiving so I continued.

I felt so trapped in my mind. I began to relive my childhood; the affairs my father had on my mother as well as the hurt and damage it caused us as a family. After the divorce, I surely hated how my mom dated married men or men going through a divorce. I despised how she put her boyfriends before her children's happiness. So, was I really just working my way to becoming her? The one who I had so long ago lost respect for? Why on earth was I choosing to become the very thing that represented my family's stronghold?

The infirmity

My thoughts ran so rampantly on a daily basis that I couldn't function properly in the things I needed to get done to advance myself as an individual. I would have full conversations with him and about him or me, but they all took place in my mind.

Even though I am very much attracted to you, I find myself shaking my head because the exact thing I held my mother hostage of, I have now fallen captive to. I don't regret any of our experiences together. I have been thinking a lot and I am possibly in a little denial. How did we get here and why am I fooling with a married man? Yet, I am still telling myself I like the way you make me feel and so this somewhat justifies it as being right. What am I getting out of this? What do I have to gain from this? Love? No, not love. Temporary pleasure… Do I hate myself that much to not think I deserve better? Why is that I can't wait for what God has for me? As I fell asleep last night I had thoughts of you with your family and wishing you were with me. I began to reflect on every time we went to our meeting spot and began to be aroused, but at the same time felt like a whore.

I tried to block those thoughts out to deny my convictions. In spite of the hard heart and the walls I had put up, I could still feel the tug of God. This made me feel that it was not too late to be restored, it was just a matter of yielding. This was easier said than done when there was so much passion between us. The way he held, touched and looked at me lingered with me. The struggle of my flesh said *I don't want to give you up*, but then the God in me replied, "*Situation is not yours to even hold onto.*"

Chapter Five
Fantasy

The letter...

"I'm not too sure you will ever know how much I care about and love you. You make me want to go there with you, but the only thing that stops me is the fact I know I can't. I also be thinking sometimes you don't want to go there w/ me anyway. I love you for who you are (and how you look... and the pussy) but you will never know that I can remain so vague sometimes b/cuz it's extremely painful for me to fight this inner battle I'm dealing with that's pulling me even more to fall in love w/ you the wrong way. I'm not very expressive (verbally) when it relates to my feelings/emotions about anything as it is, but when it comes to telling you how I really feel about you, I deliberately beat around the bush. I don't want to tell you one thing and do another, though doing otherwise is only right. If I met you when the time was right, I'd be down for whatever, no questions asked. Unfortunately, but fortunately, things did not line up like that. I don't want to hinder you, nor myself. I just want to do what's best for the both of us. I sometimes feel like I initiated separation too soon. Do you feel that way? (Usually we're flowin)

I need to know where you stand! I really feel that at this point, we need to make a decision and time is against us. I used to wish (when I first got saved) that I could be a saved lesbian. I stop feeling that way long ago until I started fucking with you. The only thing I dread thinking about is true separation. God has his own agenda; I don't want to be away from you so long that we are driven apart. I love you more than I'm allowed to show and I'm about two steps from going there.

Write me back…"

I spent exactly ten months bound with happiness and misery. My life took another unexpected turn. I was hurt and disappointed behind breaking up with the jughead of a man I had dated for less than six months.

"Why are you so hurt behind someone who obviously didn't deserve you?" Kelly asked several times in different ways.

Kelly was new to my life but it already felt like forever. I thoughtfully replied, "All the hurt is just a combination of life's disappointments and I just want all the pain to end."

She understood me and comforted me through the process. As time went on, Kelly and I laughed and joked for hours on end. She really revived me from the bad mood I existed in at that time. She had all the right words and was so compassionate. Knowing that Kelly was once a lesbian, I found myself curious about what she was like in those days, but I never could find the nerve to bring it up to her. All I knew was that I was at a point where I was so tired of the lies and games men played and I felt so safe and at ease with Kelly that I was considering propositioning her. One night, staying up late like we often did, we were talking and watching TV. The previews from *Girls Gone Wild* kept coming on and it didn't exactly help the atmosphere of curiosity and lust. We finally fell asleep and then it happened… I felt her hands down my shorts.

I don't sleep with underwear, so it kind of made for easy access. It caught me off guard at first. I wasn't sure whether to tell her to stop or keep going. I was holding my breath for a moment and then released a long pleasure-filled sigh. It felt good as her soft hands touched and rubbed me. I was fully aroused and my juices began to flow. The night went on with passionate lovemaking. I was in awe I had finally had someone who was taking me to levels sexually that no man had ever taken me before and, at the least, had an idea of how to properly dine on my tasty delicacies.

She was an expert and definitely gifted with her tongue. The experience was nothing short of splendid. Morning arrived and we made the decision that she would move in with me as my roommate. It was the perfect setup surrounding both our financial situations. I had just recently been laid off and she was trying to get away from the psychopath her mother had moved into their home. Our relationship started out so perfect and loving. The dream was so beautiful that I did not see the nightmare that was coming next.

I was enrolled in college. Kelly would help me with my homework all the time and crack jokes about my lazy brain. She fussed as she reminded me about my level of smarts and would tell me to apply myself as if she wasn't there. She would do and give me anything I asked for. Kelly always had breakfast, lunch and dinner ready daily. She kept the house immaculate, which was definitely a step up from how I used to keep it. She made up for my weakness and pampered the hell out of me. This is why I never could really understand why she betrayed me.

It was a Sunday afternoon and she would typically go to her mom's house after church. I called over to her mom's to find out how late she would be out and her mom spilled the beans. She wanted to know if Kelly and I had worked everything out. I was clueless as to what she was talking about. Finally, Kelly and I had an opportunity to talk and she told me that she would be moving out. I had mixed emotions about her moving out. I had gotten used to her being around. Nevertheless, the relationship was still fresh and new so her moving out didn't sting as bad. I guess the only thing that really angered me was she didn't have the decency to talk things over with me. I felt her move was preplanned and I was definitely being left in the dark about something. My intuition served me well, as I later learned that Kelly had laid all out on the altar with tears dripping and had spoken to several ministers regarding our relationship or, as her mom put it, *Kelly had told Minister Kachelle that she was trapped in a relationship that she didn't know how to get out of,* and that she had tried breaking things off with me, but I wouldn't let go. This was a lie.

    I was so hurt and rage-filled when I heard this. I couldn't believe it! The only thing that kept going through my mind was that passionate night and how she initiated the seed for where we were today. A week had gone by and she hadn't retrieved all her items from my apartment. My adrenalin was pumping so hard with disgust and I wanted every memory of her erased. I immediately began to pack the rest of her things and proceeded to her mom's house.

    Kelly moseyed out as usual with her nonchalant

attitude as if nothing had ever happened. The more she talked to me, the angrier I became and before I knew it I had hauled off, slapped her, and driven away like a madwoman. The next thing I knew, she was back in my life. It had been less than 24 hours since I hit her, mind you, and we were talking. It was like I had become my dad, getting my way through violence but I didn't care. In lieu of the move back to her mother's, nothing really changed except her soft body was no longer laying next to mine, but the all-night conversations and masturbation definitely made up for that. If there were gaps in her coming over, she made up for her absence each time she came to visit. After a three to four-week separation Kelly shared the news that she and her mom were being evicted.

At first I thought she would be moving back in with me, but she and her mom moved in with their cousin Sophie. To my surprise, I was invited over for Thanksgiving and it turned into me spending three nights over. One morning, Kelly and I couldn't keep our hands off of each other any longer. It was the most intense sexual experience we had ever had together. I felt like my spirit left my body and I was floating far above the clouds. I came down from my climax with my vision slightly blurry as I smiled and Kelly came up to lie next to me. She planted a kiss on my lips and then gently sucked on my nipple, causing me to explode again just as Sophie flung open the door yelling, "I knew it!"

We jumped up, grabbing our pajamas. We were fully dressed by the time Kelly's mom and other family members came to see what all the fussing and yelling was about. Sophie insisted the truth of what she saw and we actively denied it.

"This perversion can't be here in my house!" Sophie exclaimed, "Get out!" She grabbed the sheets and comforter off the bed and stormed out to shove them down into the trash bin. As I packed, I heard her saying prayers. She sounded like the mother from the movie *Carrie*. All fire and brimstone, no love in her utterances to God; we were simply vile creatures with souls in need of saving. That moment came and went, but eventually the need for Kelly and me to be together grew strong and she moved back in with me. It was also a turning point in our relationship. We had admitted to being in love with each other. It also was the very moment the devil decided he was playing for keeps.

Of course, neither of us saw this at the time but, looking back, he wanted us both dead. Our relationship had turned from love to hate. Things became unbearable between us when her biggest flaws were revealed to me. Kelly could be very fickle, and tell lies and half-truths and behave elusively. It was pure chaos, and I had begun to think I was sleeping with the enemy himself. One minute she would be so loving and the next so wicked.

Of course, I was no angel myself and I acknowledge that, but sometimes I could literally feel the spirit of evil transferring back and forth between us. I didn't have the strength to control it or denounce it. Our relationship modeled an identity crisis. One minute we wanted to be lesbians and the next minute we wanted to live for God, which we understood to mean we had to get rid of our feelings for each other. We broke up and made up so frequently that it was hard to tell when were on or off. Jealousy, rage and bitterness came upon both of us. Our relationship continued to go downhill because of the illusion we had of being in love.

Yes, I said illusion, because at that time I had come to the conclusion that there was nothing real about homosexual relationships. It was clear that Kelly and I were two people trying to fill a void of emptiness and simply did not know who we were. It was hard for either of us to admit that and neither one of us wanted to let go, even though we knew we needed to. We were determined to make it work and so we allowed it to linger and fester until we were infected. Way beyond the physical and emotional battery between us, the reality of it came at a time that we were in need of the message most.

Christmas was on the way. We had it all planned. We were going to be our own little family. We had bought a tree, decorated the apartment, and were really looking forward to a fun-filled holiday. Kelly went out Christmas shopping one night and stayed out later than we had discussed. That old beast of anger rose up within me because she hadn't called and checked in. I sat the whole Christmas tree out on the patio so it would be the first thing she saw when she drove up. To this day, I can't really tell you why I would do such a foolish act to display my frustration, although there is one thing that comes to mind, the lack of being in control. We got through our arguments about the tree being outside and her being late. Christmas finally arrived and, despite the rough patches, I was quite happy. Kelly had gotten me the most thoughtful gifts. For the first time in a long time there was peace and harmony that actually lasted for more than a day. To be exact, it lasted right up to the New Year. We had even gone to the New Year's Eve church watch service together as a couple and didn't care who saw us. Now the irony is this—it was the same church she had cried wolf at. Soon after, the harmony ended and we were back at each other's throats. Finally a breaking point came. We had an argument about something silly—a dirty dish—and I struck her. Kelly's lip bled and swelled as she declared, "Enough is enough. I want out."

"Sorry, Kelly. I didn't mean to. It's just that you know you make me so mad sometimes with all that fussing when I have had a long day. You know I love you," I offered as I went to hug her, but she pushed me away.

"I'm tired of tempting God!" Kelly blurted.

"He already warned me when I was delivered from homosexuality that if I fell back into it, the penalty would be death."

Wow, this was something, because it was then I recognized that the devil had been playing us both for fools. As far back as I could remember, the devil would whisper in my ear to terminate or at least bring some type of pain to anyone who hurt me. I knew I was capable of killing her as I watched her ice her lip, as she had done so many times before. It was satan's intentions to kill powerful women of God spiritually, mentally and physically. You would think that, having that knowledge, we both would have turned away from our sins. Don't get me wrong, we tried, but just not hard enough. My lease was scheduled to expire. We began to have conversations as to what we needed to do. It was decided that I would move from where I was because the apartment was so defiled, and she would get her own apartment.

This was the worst breakup I had ever experienced before in my life. I had constant migraine headaches, vomiting and stints of not being able to eat. The enemy was determined to take a life. I was a pure basketcase because I was so hooked on her love. Meanwhile, we supported each other as friends. We had gone apartment-hunting and she found something that she would soon call home. We were in the second week of January and the intensity grew as we awaited the end of the month. The house was quiet and I had gone to bed and left her in the living room playing on the computer. Suddenly there was a knock at the door. It was her dad, coming to move her things. I jumped up out of the bed and asked what the hell was going on. Once again I was blindsided by her lack of communication.

Kelly swore that she had told me that she would be moving in with her dad while she waited for her apartment to be ready. Of course, this sent me into a fit of rage after he left because I had been played for a fool once again. The sad thing is the deceitful spirit which was in both of us kept us moody, sporadic, and crafty. We could lie to each others' faces. know it was a lie, but yet still believe the lie. We had the biggest argument that night and, as usual, she had a way of calming me down. I know now that it was likely her self-preservation technique whereas I thought it was just her wanting to be happy. One good stroke of the tongue and her finding my G spot was all it took, and whatever I was upset about was no longer an issue. She officially moved out the next morning as I slept hard from multiple orgasms. With her dad as her support system, time passed and it was truly over between us.

    She still came over to my house to check on me from time to time. Throughout her visits she really did appear to have gotten it together, while I was still living out my drama of being hurt. One time, she invited me to join her with another friend at the mall. I could not wrap my mind around this transition she was trying to make back to us being just friends, but I agreed. I knew I wasn't completely over her and was jealous as hell because someone else was getting my time. So, it was ripe for disaster, whether I knew it or not. She didn't want to ride in the car with me. I felt that she completely ignored me the whole time we were in the mall. I was thinking, *Did you invite me here to hurt me even more?* We exchanged words and after I became violent with her in the parking lot, it was pretty much a mutual feeling that it was over. At least that's what I thought.

    Kelly finally moved into her apartment and I received a phone call from her. At first I ignored her calls, but then eventually I broke down and called her and the cycle started again. In fact I spent 90% of my time at her apartment. I only went home to change clothes and finally just started packing an overnight bag. We become inseparable again and obviously into this lifestyle deeper than anticipated. We had actually made a pact that there was no turning back now and that we would carry out every fantasy we both had. We had begun to live as man and woman. Oddly enough, Kelly took the dominant role and I liked it. We started shopping around for sex toys that would allow her the part of being male. Our sex life was really bumped up a notch when we got one. The first time we used it I believed I was really with a man. She was a pro at what she was doing to have been a first-timer with the equipment and we both enjoyed every minute of it.

    Valentine's Day was just around the corner and Kelly really went all the way out for me. She shaved all her hair off like a boy. She purchased the most beautiful white (man's) suit and had a nice red dress made for me. That night, she greeted me at the door with a dozen roses and a nice sum of cash. We dined at one of the finest restaurants in town. She treated me like a queen. Anything I wanted, she got it. The night ended and we went back to her apartment for a nightcap. The next day we took pictures and finished our Valentine weekend bash. It's funny how one weekend of fun can make up for all the wrong in a relationship.

Paradise soon came to an end, as it always did with us. The next three months was turmoil, but there was a twist. Kelly had proposed to me and gave me the most beautiful diamond ring. She began to make preparations for us to move out of state somewhere where gay marriages were recognized. She also had planned to add me to her health insurance so I could get artificially inseminated. I had never fully agreed to all of this, but because we were so in over our heads I just went with the flow.

The curveball that got thrown at us was that I let my ex-boyfriend come back into the picture. I wanted to give the relationship a second chance so I broke things off with her and attempted to work things out with him. Breaking her heart gave the old me new life. I felt that her karma had finally hit.

Kelly now had felt the pain of having the rug snatched from under her without warning. She was so hurt and now I had the upper hand. Feeling this sick sense of victory, I broke up with him and went back to her. We started a strange cycle after that of me often breaking up with her and her begging to have me back. I was the dominant one in spirit now. At some point, not being happy with this, she decided she wasn't having it and she gained control quickly. I would say our relationship was really in its last stage of do or die. We were so drained as our breakups were now occurring every other day, and both of us were taking turns to call it quits or be the one trying to hold on.

The final goodbye was on a Saturday at the end of June. I had spent all day driving around just trying to clear my head. She had company for most of the day. I eventually showed up over at her house. Everything was flowing smoothly and then when her company left she had started her chant of living for God. I am not really sure what took place that night. I want to say it was God himself that said, *Enough is enough*. I just recall having the weirdest feeling come over me. Normally, I would let her chatter and then follow up with a rebuttal, but this particular night I just walked away. Sure, I had trouble sleeping and I even called her that next morning before church. She was so belligerent in the way she spoke to me that it ruined my whole morning. I didn't even want to go to church, but I am glad I did, because deliverance came that day.

The anointing was very high that morning. Praise and worship went on longer than usual. I stood there worshiping God, but at the same time in pain behind losing my lover. The more the enemy brought her face before me, the harder I praised and went into worship. Before I knew it, I just fell to the church floor and screamed real loud and gave it to God. I felt so free after the service and was determined to stay delivered. I called my cellular provider before I had even left the church grounds and got my phone number changed, but Satan did not want to give up. The cellular network was down and the only thing the customer service agent could do for me was put the request in for a number change. So, what normally would take a second would now take 24 hours to do. I was in disarray, because I wasn't sure if I would be able to resist. Part of me really didn't expect to hear from Kelly, but I didn't want to take any chances.

Sunday evening came and went. I was in the clear. The day was just about complete and she hadn't called. Then the phone rang. It was her. I didn't answer and she went into voicemail. She had left me a message both on my cell and home phone to call her… as if yesterday or this morning had never happened. Monday morning came, my cell phone number changed, and then she began to call my home phone. I called the local telephone company and got the home number changed for 30 days, mainly because a 30-day change is free. Of course the change also took 24 hours to take effect. She continued to leave me messages both Monday and Tuesday and then I assume she finally called and got the message, *"The number you reached is no longer in service."* And that day we both stepped back into destiny. I must admit, walking away was hard and it really screwed with my intelligence that she wanted to appear to have had the capability to turn it on and off, but when the blinders came off she was just as bound as I was and didn't have control whatsoever.

    Two months later our paths crossed. It took me by surprise when I got the tap on my car window while sitting in the gas station parking lot talking on my cell phone. I looked up and it was her. She told me she had seen me driving earlier that day and was glad to know I was still alive, doing well and hadn't left the country. I tried to keep my composure, because I knew this was a test and one slip would send us right back. My conversation was short and direct. I let her know that the way things ended hurt me very bad. She replied that I had taken things the wrong way and she was just having a bad day.

For a brief moment those old feelings arose, but I finally had the strength to denounce it. I looked her straight in her eyes and told her I would always love her, but I was moving on and everything happens for a reason. After all the crying I had done I had come to the realization that it was better this way and I was cool with it. As I drove away from her, there was so much relief to have passed that test. A couple of months had gone by and I was truly feeling free, but the devil just kept plotting and scheming. My task now was learning to ignore.

I had so many people coming to me telling me that Kelly was walking around her church pointing all fingers back to me. She was the innocent one was the lie she had put out. Her mother had told me the two of them had a big argument because Kelly felt her mother had chosen me over her. Her mother went on to tell me that she explained to Kelly that she didn't choose one over the other, it was the fact that God had shown her that true deliverance would come by way of me. Kelly's mom went on to say how she let her daughter know that she had walked through this lifestyle with her before so there was not much to be said.

She told Kelly she held on to me because I came to her and told her what we had been into, exactly how God showed her I would do. Kelly had become hostile, according to her mom, and even alluded to the fact that it was me who didn't want to let go. I was angry once again as I had been previously when she tried to paint this picture. A part of me wanted to get revenge because I was just tired of the stupidity, but the God in me gave me such peace. I had hurt so many people while I was bound with this spirit and I took full responsibility for it. In fact, I knew I had to go back to each one of those people and apologize, starting with my spiritual fathers, mentors and friends. My peace came from telling what I did and why it was so hard to walk away. As I gave my apology and testimony I kept her covered.

I had come to think that I could take the coward's way out and say that if she had never touched me that first night, I wouldn't have got caught up, but the truth is—it was no one's fault. Either one of us could have walked away from it much earlier, before it had gotten out of control, but we didn't. We made a conscious decision to stay in it. God had provided us with so many ways of escape, but we decided to ride on mercy and grace. Don't get me wrong, it was a stronghold that was very hard to loosen. There comes a time in life when you have to recognize things for what they are. We were two women of God who enjoyed shooting the breeze with each other and pushing each other to the next spiritual level. So what would I have to gain by tearing her down?

Regardless of all the pain and sin, she is still part of the body of Christ and that connects her to me. So when she bleeds, I bleed. Yes, it has been very difficult for me to speak blessings over her life. It was hard to celebrate when I would get wind of good news regarding her. I still keep her lifted and have the highest respect for her, despite the negative words others tell me she speaks about me. God has really taught me and I am still learning that true deliverance is when you stop pointing the finger out, and begin to point it in and still bless those who wrong you.

Chapter Six
Dirty

And here we go…

"Let me just say it's been a blast. When I talk to you as of lately, you feel as though you have so much to get together that it's not even funny. Our last deepest conversation was about a certain issue. And you said… well, you would straighten it out on your end and I would do the same, but today you admitted that we are just friends. The hardest part is that feelings are there, but how you are is starting to dwindle. You're limited in speech and actions toward me and that makes me feel awkward. That's the third time you've just vanished and I haven't heard anything—that leaves a person wondering. I'm getting myself together as well, but I guess your definition of getting self wellness means partial and/or total abandonment. I don't know, if you let something go and it comes back then it was meant to be, if not, life goes on. I'm getting mixed emotions because of how you are talking to me. It's like you are being elusive. I guess one day everything will be brought in focus. I'm learning every day about life, love, friends, loved ones, and just being alive. My dad used to always say, 'There is no such thing as friends.' You know, sometimes I believe that based on how people treat me. I may not mean much in your eyesight, but I'm still somebody. I have a lot more to say, but time is drawing nigh and I have to get up early tomorrow; maybe you will finally believe, trust and learn me; moreover, talk to me."

I crumpled the letter up while thinking, *Nigga, please, have you lost your mind? "You may not mean much in my eyesight, but you are still somebody." You got that right. You are somebody—somebody's husband.*

It all started a year prior to this ridiculous letter. I was sitting on my couch, feeling lonely and, quite frankly, I was horny. I had just finished rubbing my breasts and was snaking my hand down my abdomen toward my clit when I heard a hard knock on the door. I jumped. The familiar thuds seemed like the police just before they kick your door open. Of course, why I know that is part of this big story of my life. I looked around the room like a frightened kitten. I don't know why I did. I no longer had people in my life who were prone to bringing illegal things in my home. I quickly washed my hands as another knock bounced sound off the walls inside.

"I will be right there!" I called out.

I rushed over to the door, peeked through the peephole and saw nothing. I opened the door and a flier hit the floor. I looked up and saw the silhouette of a tall man sticking a flier in another door at the end of the hall and then disappearing. I was partially angry but amused at myself for all the thoughts that had run through my mind before opening that door. I picked up the flier and almost tore it up, but I glanced over it first. It had a coupon on it for discounted moving services. I certainly was tired of the hassle of moving alone and knew I would be planning to go at the end of my lease. I locked the door, put it in my coupon drawer and thought, *Now, where was I?* I went right back to it with no interruptions and I slept solidly after.

As time went on, I thought little of the flier or the shadow of the man. There was nothing to know or see, not even from the flier. My life was actually too chaotic for me to care. Shit was happening daily. For instance, there was the catalyst that led me right to him. When you live in an apartment, no matter how solid the walls, you can often hear what's going on next door. Sometimes what you hear is entertaining, erotic, annoying, or completely maddening. I had grown used to the life of my neighbors, because what I heard was familiar.

Anger one moment, then all flirts and giggles the next. I would see him and her here and there, nothing extensive but just enough to recognize them and say hello. One time, while in the complex laundry room, I saw her but her hello was muffled and spiritually distant. I looked at her, wondering what it was about. We almost were dancing in there with the lengths it seemed she went to in order to not present her full self to me; however, her natural kindness foiled her plan of avoidance. I accidentally knocked over my liquid detergent and we both grasped at it, knowing how pricey a thing it is to spill out. She grabbed it first and handed it to me. As I thanked her, I noticed the problem quickly.

"What happened to your face? It was him, wasn't it?" I asked knowingly. "Nothing, it was just a little love tap. It will get better soon," she responded, in such a way that told she had said this to someone else in her life many times before. "It's none of my business, but you know there are places you can go, right, to be safe?" I asked in a somewhat prompting tone as I noticed her folding the last of her laundry more quickly.

"I know and I have been to one. He is working on it. Thanks for your concern," she said and then she was on her way out before I could say another thing.

I couldn't get her off my mind. Well, really, I couldn't get my mom and dad off my mind. The more I heard the neighbors arguing, the more upset I would get. Most nights I tossed and turned as I felt like a kid again, in my room, just wanting it all to stop. I started looking for apartments, but wanted it to be the right one where the residents are sifted out and screened well. I even considered buying a house but wasn't ready for that step. My process to moving out was suddenly accelerated due to the events that took place one night. I heard a lot of yelling and agonizing screams. I pressed my ear against my bedroom wall to hear better.

"You fucking whore! Whose is it?" he demanded. Sobbing, she responded, "No one else. The baby is yours! I swear it!" Unyielding in his rage, he yelled, "It's a lie! You know I had a vasectomy!"

"I don't understand. I thought you'd be happy. It's a miracle. You said you had been praying for one since before we even met. Why wouldn't you believe it when it happens?" she questioned through tears.

On hearing that, I thought about how people often do exactly what she said.

They speak of miracles but don't believe them. Vasectomies do have a failure rate. I thought their argument would die down and I relaxed a bit, thinking she was right and he would just plan on a paternity test at some point… and just be happy. However, that's not what happened. I heard the sound of him slamming her against the wall. When I heard her pleading with him to stop, begging him not to risk losing the baby, I couldn't take it anymore. I have no clue why I didn't just call the police. I had enough. I looked under my bed and reached for my shoebox of old things. I wished I still had my gun, but what I had would be enough. I slipped the set of brass knuckles on my fingers and stretched my hands out, briefly looking at these old friends that got me out of many jams. I took a deep breath, thinking, *Here goes nothing.*

I went next door and could still hear the carrying on. I knocked. There was a brief silence. I heard him tell her to stay right where she was or he would kill her. I knocked again and heard his approaching footsteps. I put my decorated fists behind me. He opened the door, leaving the chain on.

In a threatening voice he asked, "What do you

want?"

"Is your wife home? I told her I would help her out with something," I responded in a cool, collected way.

He glared at me as if he knew. "She's busy," he declared. I could tell he was about to close the door. All those daily squats I would do for added sexiness were about to come in handy for strength too. The adrenalin surged through me as I took a brief squat and launched the flat of one of my feet into the door with great force. The chain snapped right off, causing the door to hit him. So much for added security. The expression on his face was scarier than any thing I had seen, but I didn't care.

He launched himself at me and took one straight to the jaw. The gash pleased me and I got excited. I convinced myself that I was being the hero that no one ever was for my family. I wish he had been knocked out but he was still coming after me. I would find different ways to dodge him and still hurt him. I could hear her screaming about what was taking place. I had just gotten the best of him. He was rolling on the ground, writhing in pain. I wasn't sure what I was going to do next, but I was interrupted by the anger fog disappearing and me processing her words. I almost thought I was hearing wrong, but I wasn't.

"Stop it! You are hurting him! Get out of here!" she yelled and then she started throwing stuff from around the apartment at me.

Say what? If there was ever a *what-the-fuck* moment, that was it. She, standing there with a bloodied face, and possibly a soon-to-be miscarriage, wanted me to stop. I raised my hands up like in a surrender to the police and backed up as she held onto the item she was about to throw. She dropped it and then ran to his aid.

"You people need help," I said as I continued backing away and returned to my apartment.

I didn't sleep that night, wondering what would happen next. I do know they left almost right away, likely to get him stitched up. I thought the police would be showing up, but they didn't. Judging by the scenario, I pictured him as a man of vengeance and knew I needed to get out fast. As soon as the leasing office opened for one of the places I had been interested in, I contacted them and moved through the process quickly. Money talks, and for a change I had some to spend. I only had a month left on the current lease and so I would just let it run out unlived in. I came back and started packing like a madwoman.

While doing so, I remembered the flier for the

moving company. I scrambled for it and opened it like it was salvation itself. I called and said that I needed an emergency move and I would pay extra. The man who was once only a fleeting shadow down the hall answered and said he would be over right away because he had no appointments for that day. It was *right on time*, as he put it.

When he arrived, I thought *Oh my, he is gorgeous*, but I did not pursue him in an emergency moment like that, although I surely considered it. We talked business and then he began to flirt with me. I kept it professional and was excited to learn that he would finish all the packing for me and get it to the new apartment. I gave him the address and explicit instructions that, no matter who asks him, he is not to share my new address. He joked about me being under witness protection and I made every effort not to give away my nervousness about the thought of it. I felt like I might need some sort of service like that. Not because I was scared but because I didn't want to give in to that demon that would convince me to just kill the neighbor.

I waited for him at the new place and everything went off without a hitch. He and a couple of other moving men arrived and got the items in quickly. The whole time I watched him. He just looked so good. As late afternoon grew into evening, they wrapped it up. The other men were putting their supplies in the truck when he came over to me. He was close and I inhaled the scent of cologne, which I didn't expect after he had gotten all that work done. I felt a light throb in my clit and readjusted my legs, squeezing them slightly together to make it go away.

"I want to thank you for the business. Not enough people support us, you know." He slid his finger along the back of his hand to indicate that he was talking about the support of black businesses, but all I could do was picture that long finger getting me hot and ready to receive him.

Calmly I replied, "Oh, think nothing of it." I took a couple of twenty-dollar bills out and tried to pass it to him as a tip, but he raised his hand up.

"Why don't you keep that? That way, I won't be using your money when I take you out to lunch tomorrow," he said.

I looked at him, shocked yet intrigued. I wondered if he had noticed me lusting after him earlier. This was a strange turn in the conversation. I didn't know if I wanted it or didn't.

"I am sorry, no can do," I responded.

He grinned at me in a way that softened me. My

words to him should have been goodnight, but instead I asked him if was he was married. He held up his bare left hand with a smile. That action meant nothing to me, so I asked him again and he said yes, but explained that they had been having problems. I told him that I was not interested in being involved with a married man. He said okay and I thought that was the end of that. However, he pursued me like never before. He called often to say he was just checking on me and even sent me flowers.

    I eventually accepted a lunch date with him, not because I wanted the company but because I was actually hungry that day. I was short on cash from all the moving expenses and a surprise car repair shortly after. When I accepted the lunch date, we both agreed that our interactions would be strictly platonic. Our platonic relationship lasted for about one month and in the bed we went.

    The first time we were together sexually, it was definitely the furthest thing from my mind. I was fed up with my car and all its troubles. I advertised it for sale *As Is* so I could get some money to use as a down payment on an up-to-date car, but I was concerned that the potential buyer seemed sketchy over the phone.

    He had asked me several peculiar questions,

including whether any of the men in my home would be present. He said he would be paying in cash, though, and I really wanted to sell. I told him yes and gave him the information. I had heard too many stories about sales turned to robberies and I didn't want to look like I lived alone based on his questions, so I asked him, my platonic friend, to come over. He gladly took on the responsibility of being present but was having a bit too much fun in pretending to be my boyfriend in front of the buyer.

From sliding his arm around my waist to gentle kisses planted on my neck, it was becoming too much for there to be someone present while I was getting hot. The affection was all unnecessary, though, because it turned out that the buyer only asked about the men being present because he was a devout Islamic man who didn't typically conduct business with the woman of the house. Learning this, at least my friend stepped up to conduct all the business so I could get the money, but he also had too much fun "ordering" me to go inside while the men negotiated. I passed him the paperwork and keys as I rolled my eyes at him and went upstairs to watch them from the balcony.

I saw the deal get completed and he headed up to me with the funds. I opened the door and thanked him.

He slyly replied with an *Anything for you, baby*. It sounded like silk when he said that. I quivered a bit as I took the money from him. I went to the kitchen counter with it and started organizing and counting it. He told me that it was all there and I explained that I just like organizing my cash by denomination and having it all facing the same way. It was an old cashier habit.

As I counted, he walked up behind me and wrapped his arms around my waistline while kissing me on the neck. I was done. I actually came in that one action. It must have already had been building up in me but I was in denial of it. I turned and we started kissing, all the while I was getting wetter and trembling as I wanted more. I wanted him inside of me badly but also wanted to relish in every touch. I excitedly reached into his pants and felt his dick.

The head was sticky with pre-cum and I was disappointed, hoping that he knew how to control himself. Within a few seconds, I realized it wasn't the only issue. His tool didn't feel big at all. I thought I was missing something. I wanted to get a closer look and so I squatted to pull down his pants. The big mistake was he thought that position meant I was going to suck his dick. I looked at it and almost laughed. My eyes stretched wide at the sight of his weird uncircumcised penis, which looked like a turtle's head peeking out ever so slightly. Thinking I didn't know much about them and maybe sucking would help, I went against my principles and gave it the gift of my tongue. It didn't grow any bigger than that. It was four to five inches at best.

Just when I wasn't going to give him the dignity of continuing, he pulled me to standing and picked me up, placing me on the counter. He spread my legs and worked his tongue all around my clit in just the right way. In that moment I had forgotten all about his penis, which is probably what he had hoped I would do. After what was surely my third orgasm of the afternoon, he kissed me in a long trail from clit to lips. We shared a passionate kiss and then he entered me.

I couldn't feel it but I knew he was in there by the way he was moving his hips. I thought to myself, *Is this really it? How can a man who looks so damned fine have nothing to offer down below?* I screamed at myself, *What are you doing? Forget the size of it. He is married! You have been down this road before and you felt miserable afterwards.* Five minutes went by and he came with his entire being. He looked like he was having a seizure. I couldn't believe it. I was in some strange funhouse on a street between the five-minute brother cliché that turned out to be true and Gillette's *Short Dick Man*. I had opened my legs for an "extra belly button" on that day and many days after. *What was wrong with me?*

The more time we spent together, the more I ignored all the red flags that were there. I knew it was a setup from the devil but ignored it. Who had I been kidding? I was aware that I didn't like the guy in a sexual way and that most of the time I was just going through whatever motions necessary in order to climax. It was always better when someone else did it instead of me. I continued the "friendship" with him, though it was clear we had nothing in common. Along the way, I discovered he was a very vain person. I suppose it made him feel good to accentuate the positive, his face and toned muscles, but eliminate the negative... too small to even speak further about.

One evening after another obligatory spreading of my legs after he had overcompensated with oral sex, he kissed me more than usual and was overly affectionate.

"I am in love with you," he told me in a very dedicated tone that I wasn't buying.

Tossing back my head in laughter, I replied, "You are not. You are in love with the idea of being with me."

"Do you love me?" he questioned with almost a puppy dog's whimper. I gave him a hard Cruella de Vil,

"No!"

What an idiot! How do you fall in love with someone that you hardly know?

Someone whom you only had lunch with once and all the rest of the time spent together is sexual? I guess that makes me an idiot too, though, both in past relationships and now. I was in no way sexually attracted to him nor were we compatible. We were into our third month by this point and all I had was broken promises, thirty dollars for my birthday gift and two trips to the doctor behind a bacterial vaginosis infection. He tried to insist that it had to be me, but I was sure it wasn't. We had arguments about it and when it cleared up, I still had not gotten a clue. I surely was lonelier than I admitted and had little value in myself because I still found myself with him with my legs up in the air.

The cycle didn't stop until he called me because he had been experiencing a burning sensation when he peed and a smelly discharge in between. He went to the doctor about it. This time, it was trichomoniasis. He was panicking since his lie had come to the forefront. It was obvious that he was still sleeping with his wife even though he kept claiming otherwise. Now he was calling me scared and apologizing. I had nothing to say to him and just hung up. I was in a way relieved, because I had tried to break things off with him a couple times and he wouldn't take no for an answer. He knew how to use words that would make me feel loved and wanted, yet another quiet longing from childhood.

Some days went by and I thought I didn't have the infection at first. I felt fine until I smelled something terrible. I kept looking around, thinking there was a mouse somewhere and it had died. When I went to use the restroom, I realized the smell I was hunting down was actually me. My vaginal discharge was toxic, with a smell like ammonia and old dumpster trash combined. I thought a good bath would help but it did not. Another day went by and I had air fresheners all over the house. I was so scared to have unexpected company, it wasn't even funny. Talk about drama! *Was the dick really worth the inconvenience and discomfort?*

I gave in and went to the doctor. The visit was horrible. I dressed up very sharply as I always did when things weren't going my way. I could have been on the cover of *Emerge* magazine. There I was thinking, *I am just the bomb* (cute, if you don't know the term) but by the look on everyone's faces, the smell would blow anyone away. I guess my plan didn't work. I had put an air freshener in each of my pants pockets. People actually were scooting away and there was this kid who just kept staring at me. At one point, because kids are always brutally honest, he looked at me and said, "You smell like my cat's poop tray." Just then my name was called and I was so glad to go in.

I could hear the nurse spraying the hallway after the door to the exam room closed. When the doctor came in, he said, *Excuse me a moment*, and quickly put on a mask before he went through a series of questions:

- Are you pregnant or nursing at this time?

- How many partners have you had?

- Do you know what protection is and do you use it?

- Do you engage in anal sex?

- Have you ever been tested for STDs, including HIV?

He answered the fifth on his own, casually stating, "No need to answer that. I forgot you were just here two months ago for a similar problem."

When the exam was over, I was given a

prescription. I was angry because I knew I had welcomed this Negro into my bed. I could not stand the smell of myself spiritually or physically, but it didn't send me to a prayer closet either. I sat back scheming on all the ways I could get back at him. My reason for wanting to hurt him was not because our relationship ended the way it did, but because I didn't even see him as a person anymore. He was another representation of my pain in life. I wondered how his wife was so in the dark as her husband would come to my house when he was supposed to be at work. It just made me sick to my stomach how a man could use the word 'love,' but still make unwise choices that leave people hurting.

    I drove past his home and I got his license plate number from his car. I did a seven-year background check on him and found everything out about him… *Indecent liberties with a minor!* I could see that it was only a high-school girl that likely lied about her age to begin with, but still, I was ready to destroy him, the reputation of his business and everything he loved. That was the part that stopped me from doing it. He loved nothing more than his children. It was the one thing I had learned about him and probably what kept me drawn in. I pictured his children not having their father and what would happen next if they had no one to look after them while their mom worked. I got a flash of my neighbor's son telling me to do those things to him. It was in that memory that I took the higher road and just walked away.

Though he moved on with his life, I spoke to him again just to share my feelings of anger with him because I needed to do that to move on as well. His only response was, "It is a thorn in my flesh and I shall be delivered from it." *What the hell kind of excuse is that?* This was a definite lesson on keeping my panties on and understanding that what looks nice ain't always nice. You would think I would have made him wear a condom after the first time but, better yet, since I was so deep off into church, you would think I would have just kept my legs closed until God sent me a husband OF MY OWN.

Chapter Seven
Realization

There came a point for me where I felt that, in order to really have a handle on my anger, I needed an outlet. So, I chose to take a creative writing course on Saturdays. Writing felt good and I especially enjoyed those entries where we wrote in our private journals about anything we wanted for 15 minutes. The professor was not very much older than me. She was so confident and creative. I hung on her every word and pictured myself in her place, teaching others to become centered as they flowed through life. One day, when she returned one of my papers, she left a sticky note on it that said to set up a conference with her by calling the department secretary. I wondered what it was all about since I was only taking an enrichment course—I wasn't a formal student or anything.

The meeting took place on a Monday. I entered her office rather timidly. I don't know why but I felt see-through being this up close and personal with the woman whom I had been admiring. She invited me to close the door and sit down,

"I asked you here today because I wanted to talk to you about your writing…"

I interrupted her, "Why? Is it that bad? Do I have to drop the course?"

"No, quite the contrary," she affirmed with a quick laugh, "I think your writing is brilliant. I was wondering if the content in your recent assignment is a work of fiction or from your real life?"

"A mixture of both, actually," I responded hesitantly, still waiting for her to drop some bad news on me.

"That is fascinating. Not unheard of, but fascinating. I would like to see you more at campus and, in my spare time, help you to develop a collection of your stories and poems. I know a few publishers who might be interested in your voice and what you have to share with the world. How would you feel about that?" she asked.

"I am not sure. This was just a hobby, to help me work through some stuff," I said.

"Understood, but sometimes sharing with more than just yourself is a gift to yourself and others. Think about it and, if you are ready, we can get started as early as next week. Just call the secretary again to set things up," she stated.

We said our goodbyes for the day and I went home to think about it. I also suddenly had writing fever. I sat down and my pen kept moving across the page until I had completed a deeply therapeutic poem:

I Realized

I realized
I used to be self-centered.
I didn't care who I hurt.
I always wanted things my way;
there was never a grey area
only black and white.
If you didn't jump when I said jump
I felt betrayed and hurt.
Yet I had the nerve to tell people
NO when I felt like it.
Whenever something happened,
it was never my fault.
I always shift the blame.
There was always something wrong
with someone else.
NOT ME!

At one point in my life,
I decided I would set so-called boundaries.
I'm not going to let anyone else run over me. (I said)
I had developed a no-nonsense attitude. (Yeah right)
I was very arrogant and anal.
In fact my favorite cliché was
"Ain't nobody I got to have."
I felt I could never let anyone close to me.
(You know, protect the heart)
Then one day I realized
it wasn't everyone else's fault.
I realized
it was my fault.
I pushed people away
because I was afraid of getting hurt.
I had a big mouth
not to be heard, but to seem tough.
I was very selfish;
I felt the world owed me something
for the pain I had been through
in my past.
Then I realized
the person I was really angry
and afraid of was me.
I realized the only person

who owed me anything was me.
Then I gave my life to Christ;
in my renewal, God began to clean me up.
I realized
in order for the pain to go away,
I had to face myself and once I did that,
forgiving others would be easier.
I realized
it wasn't everyone else stopping me from growing
IT WAS ME
I realized
God had been trying to get my attention
for quite some time,
but because I was so defensive,
I wouldn't listen.
I realized
God wanted to heal my heart,
but because I was so bitter,
I wouldn't give him the key.
I realized
all cares must be cast upon Him.
I realized as a Christian
I must continue to love those who wrong me.
I realized
man will fail me and God will not.

I realized
the world doesn't revolve around me.
I realized
I must appreciate those
who have my best interest at heart,
even when they are not available for me
or tell me no at times.
I've realized
I have to love unconditionally,
not conditionally.
I've learned to evaluate each situation
and not make rash
decisions and cut people out of my life.
I realized
that in my Christian walk, I might stumble.
However, I'm not afraid anymore;
because I know God's heavenly angels
are right there to catch me.
I'm not afraid to hurt because I know
God only wants to strengthen me.
I realized
that I hurt God every day,
but he doesn't abandon me.
Therefore, what right do I have to abandon others?
I realized

that God wants me to be like a child,
so humble and innocent.
Nevertheless, as I wear my flesh
I am an adult.
I finally realized it's time for me to
take responsibility for my actions.
I realized
that I'm not
perfect.

When I was done, I was ready for the next calling in my life, which was put directly in my face by the professor. I felt filled with light and thought nothing could ever take it from me again, but, again, I was to discover how wrong I was. The chase for my soul returned more easily than I thought it would. I had been working with the professor for months and was even invited a couple of times to share my writings aloud with the full-time students at the school. After a reading that I dedicated to Mariah, I found myself crying and excused myself.

I sat outside under a tree. As I wiped my face, wondering why I was allowing myself to be so vulnerable before strangers, a student who had followed me from the classroom came to me and asked me a question.

"Do you believe in miracles?" I was a bit confused and stuttered slightly, "Of course. God can do anything beyond our imagination."

"What if I told you that your friend Mariah is alive and well, not dead like you wrote in your story?" the peculiar girl beamed.

"Well, of course it is possible. I never knew for sure but I wrote based on what I guessed her outcome was. When we don't keep up with people in life, their story can only be what we imagine until we learn the truth," I said.

"She goes to my church. I know it is her because she told a testimony story that matches yours and has said your name, wondering where you are," the girl stated.

"I am sorry, but I think you are mistaken. I am not even from around here," I said, brushing it off and wanting her to go.

"Neither is she. She's not from here and she said that she had a fight in the streets with her best friend and it was the fight, plus the friend yelling at her to get help that haunted her each day that she spent in the streets until she changed," the girl reaffirmed, now looking more angelic than when she first spoke.

I knew she was telling the truth because, of all the writing I shared, I had not shared anything about the fight to the people in that classroom. I only detailed Mariah's addiction and what her physical change had been.

"Come to prayer meeting tomorrow. She never misses. It's the Metropolitan Community Church over on Nettle Blvd. and 8th St. It starts at 6 p.m.," she said, before returning to class. I had never heard of the church but I wanted to go. I just had to see if it was true and my long-lost friend was there and, even better, walking in the Light. I barely slept and was all nerves as I wondered what would happen when we saw each other? What would we do? What would we say?

When I arrived at the church, I had not expected what I found there. It was different than anything I had seen. I was welcomed and felt at ease among the multiracial congregants. I felt as though I was with friends. It took me a while to notice it, but as I looked from chatty group to chatty group, I realized that several of them were same-sex couples. They were hand in hand, and no one seemed to care. Some of them even had children. *What is this place?* I wondered. I didn't see Mariah anywhere but I did see the girl from class. I walked up to her and she explained that Mariah was the church secretary as well, and arrives last after she getting her baby from the childcare room. Baby?

Mariah is a mother? The young lady told me that I should probably wait over at the childcare room and I would end up catching Mariah before she entered the sanctuary. I followed her directions and waited there after she had properly introduced me to the childcare director. I looked at all the children, wondering which one was Mariah's. I thought it would be an easy guess, but so many looked ethnically mixed just like her. Mother after mother picked up their child and I didn't have to guess much longer because eventually there was only one left.

She was gorgeous and no more than a few months old. She cried and the childcare director nurtured her, assuring the little baby that one of her mommies would be along soon. Yet another question was answered. Mariah still enjoyed women like I once had but how did she have a baby? Was it natural or medical-assisted? My head started to hurt. Just when I was about to give up and leave, Mariah rushed in and apologized for being late, easily taking the baby into her arms. Seeing her there, healthy and with her hair longer than I remembered, she looked like the Madonna and Child painting that I had so often seen in different versions over the years. She smiled, and damn it if my heart didn't skip a beat against my will.

"Mariah, you've had a guest waiting for you here," the director said, nodding toward me.

"You have got to be kidding me? Are you really in front of me right now?" Mariah said in disbelief and joy.

The director told Mariah that she would leave us

to talk and to please remember to set the alarm before coming to the sanctuary.

"There was a student at the college where I take Creative Writing. When I told a story, she put two and two together... How did you end up here?" I asked.

She explained how it was a long story involving a rehab program and a church mission trip that changed her entire direction and landed her here. She told me that she thought I had probably died, which was strange considering that was what I thought about her. What about me would make her think I would be dead? After I got over my offense and judging, I stopped kidding myself and recognized exactly why she would think such athing, choking back all the smart-aleck things I almost said.

We chatted more and she invited me to prayer service and the dinner that they always had there on Wednesdays. She said that her wife was in the hospitality ministry and helped cook almost all the food. She told me I was in for a treat. I don't know why my heart sank to hear it, because I wasn't like that anymore. As we walked to the sanctuary, I couldn't help but ask why everyone at this church was cool with gay relationships. Weren't they afraid of God's wrath? She told me MCC embraces everyone and promotes both spirituality and love. As I never heard of it, I was surprised to hear that it had churches all over the world. Mariah further explained that it was all about interpretations and they believed that most people are breaking down the word of God in the wrong way. According to her, it was too much to get into right now.

I really felt like leaving. I didn't want to hear about anything that tore down everything I was raised to believe in, everything that I knew was right. However, I still wanted to be with her a little more. So, I attended the prayer service. It was so calm and loving in there, I had to admit. I felt as though I wanted to stay there in that peace forever. I even began to wonder if I could get over their beliefs on homosexuality and resist it at the same time. When it was over, I talked to Mariah and averted my eyes as she suddenly started breastfeeding. Again another question answered, but how? After all these years, she could still read my face. She told me that she and her wife invested in IVF, then went on and on about how much they loved each other and it all happened kind of fast.

"Enough about me, tell me about you. What has happened since we have been apart? Are you married? Any kids?" she rambled as she finally put the breast away.

I answered a few of her questions in as light a way as possible so that I didn't have to reach back into my pain for this unexpected reunion. We walked to the fellowship hall and went through the line. Once seated, we prayed, thanked God for the miracle of us being together again, and started eating. The food was delicious. I tasted so familiar and comforting.

Just as I was taking another big bite, probably too big for public eating, I heard Mariah say, "Here comes my wife now."

I actually started choking when I saw that Mariah's wife was Kelly. Someone nearby patted my back, when they really should have just let me die then for all the trouble that took place next. I stood up with more fury in me than I had ever had. Mariah and her baby barely got out of the way as I mountain-climbed over the table and jumped on Kelly, calling her every name I could think of under the sun. We were rolling and tussling; striking each other repeatedly just like old times and, like the old times, she was not stronger than me. It took three men using all of their strength to pull me off her. I would have ripped her hair from her head had she not been wearing that damn buzzcut again.

I kept cursing her out as they held onto me. Kelly was not even focused on me. She was just over at

Mariah and seemingly explaining how we knew each other. I wanted to fight more and people in the room started praying, some were speaking in tongues. I felt myself yielding to the prayers that I didn't want to hear. I didn't want to be calmed down and the next thing I knew I was crying. It was a cry from the deepest pit of my belly, harboring all of the poison of my past. It was what people commonly call the ugly cry. Tears, snot, drooling, all of it and, without warning, there was nausea and vomiting. At first I didn't understand it but the group started saying Amen and Thank you, Father as I threw up.

I figured out after a moment that they believed the sickness had been sending the demons within me packing. I won't even dispute that now, because I had an overwhelming feeling of peace as the police officers arrived at the fellowship hall to arrest me. The cuffs were placed on me and, as I walked away, I heard Mariah say, "We forgive you," followed by Kelly, and then others offering the same chorus in rounds. We forgive you.

I didn't call anyone to bail me out. I only had to stay 72 hours in the end, but I desperately needed that time. I read the bible and talked to God in a way I never had before. I started forgiving everyone and myself. I asked for direction and help. I surrendered. On the day I was released, I knew everything truly would be different. I felt new because it was by God's work and not my own attempts to create newness in me. I became hungry for His word and focused on what He would have me do with my life story to help others. The more I did so, the more my life became great. However, knowing what I know now, I wonder why I even expected that there would never be another trial set to my weaknesses. What a doozy it would

Chapter Eight
Disturbia

For the many years that I battled my anger, feeling I could take someone's life in an instant to appease myself, something always held me back from the fate that would come with such a choice.

Every morning before starting my day, I would pray and girt up in the full armor of God. I thought I had a full handle on it until God showed me what still lurked beneath. A lady at work by the name of Ronnie was antagonizing me to no avail. Every opportunity she got she would point out my faults, always sarcastically stating, "And you are a Christian."

I noticed that when I was reading my bible every day it was easy for me to ignore her, and I often found myself in the women's restroom, crying out to God for her. I truly was praying for my enemy, but it all changed when I began to operate outside the will of God. Even though I was attending church, I had stopped reading my bible and, before I knew it, my personal time with God had stopped. I gave away his time to the TV mostly and, when not that, it was shopping, beauty treatments, and going to social events to try to impress people who didn't even know me and vice versa. With all of that neglect of my relationship with Him, I found myself often distressed and the attacks from the devil seemed overwhelming. I was no longer in surrender. I was controlling my life and receiving the outcomes that go with it. All matters were taken into my own hands.

The problem with Ronnie was the absolute epitome of it. I went to outright war with Ronnie. There was constant bickering, but I still had convictions. So, I would go back and apologize to her and then turn right back around and open up a can of whoop-ass on her. I couldn't for the life of me figure out why she hated me or what she felt she had on me. I had got so far off focus that I began to consume every minute of my day trying to get even. It had gotten so bad that, instead of ending a day's work and leaving work at work, I had found myself bringing the problem home. I would spend endless time discussing her with family and friends while she was probably at home not losing a bit of sleep.

I had lost all concept of who I was in Christ. I walked into the office one morning as if she didn't exist. I had said hello to everyone except her, and when our paths crossed in the hallway I looked her right in the eye and didn't utter a word. The whole day, I intentionally did things that would make her work tasks last longer or have clients angry at her for various things I had orchestrated. As I passed her I could feel the cries for help in her spirit, but I was so full of strife that I did not care. My attitude was horrible. I snapped at people when they tried to tell me that I was being petty and needed to be the bigger person.

I wasn't interested in hearing that type of advice. I just wanted to get even. One day, after she had clocked out, I went into the employee records and found her address. I was going to take it to the streets in order to shut it down. I pulled up in front of her home and watched, like I was on a stakeout. I saw her pass the window here and there but couldn't tell if she lived alone. I decided to get out and do what I was there for. I hoped it wouldn't come down to something physical, but I would beat her ass if I needed to. When I got to her door, I rang the bell. There was no answer. I rang it several more times and she didn't come to the door.

"Bitch, do you think you can ignore me? I already saw you inside. Come on out!" I invited. "You want to talk so much shit at work, see me now."

The door opened and she stood there with a shotgun in hand.

"Shut the fuck up and get in here. You aren't going to do a damned thing to anybody." She let me know that she wasn't playing as she placed the barrel directly on my forehead. She backed up as I stepped in.

"Close the door!" she commanded.

I closed the door. She kept the gun aimed at me but backed away. I wanted to disarm her, but for the life of me I couldn't remember how to do it as my dad had taught me. I did remember that he told me that one mistake could cause me to be the one to lose my life. So I didn't act. She told me to sit down.

"You really don't know who I am, do you?" she asked.

"You arrogant Christians are all the same. You get saved, bury your past, and pretend to be better than everyone… always judging."

I barely looked at her at work, but the more I was forced to look at her now and observe her face, I realized exactly who she was, and I was the biggest jackass on the planet. Ronnie was my neighbor Terry's youngest sister. When I still lived at home with my mother, I saw Terry bringing her home from her school dance. He pulled up into their driveway, much further in than usual, but I thought nothing of it until I heard her muffled yells saying,

"Terry, stop! No! What are you doing?" I went to see what was going on.

She saw me and directly yelled for me to help her. It was clear he was groping her in the car and overpowering her. I stood there frozen, watching, and not responding to her at all. I shook my head no and backed away slowly. Just when he started raping her, I disappeared. The next morning, unlike me, she had ignored his threats and told her mother when she returned from her third shift job. The police were called and a rape kit was used. They considered the results inconclusive. It was her word against his. He claimed that she was a fast girl and had given it up to some boy at the dance.

The police asked about witnesses and she told them how I had been standing right there and saw the whole thing. When they came to my house to ask, I denied having seen a thing. I said that I wasn't even home. I had broken her heart because I was her only hope. Her mother believed Terry's story and mistreated her from then on out, while he continued to have his way with her. She came to me several times after and pleaded with me, pretty much all the way up until I moved out with Joe at my mother's demand.

Years later, when I was about to move and wanted

to claim a few of my things that remained behind at my mother's house, I saw her and asked her to come over to me. She did so and I quietly apologized for not saying what I knew. I told her Terry had forced me to do things and other people had done the same to me. I explained that I was in so much pain that I didn't know how to react. I also mentioned that the rule of the street is snitches get stitches and I had no intention of getting that fate at the time. I offered her my new address and told her that if she wanted to get away from it all to come see me. She took the address and went into her place. It took her some time, but one day she showed up.

    Unfortunately, she showed up into madness and I didn't receive her well at all. I thought she was going to ruin everything. She looked like the devil to me, standing there with her perfect body and face. I saw her only as temptation for my man. I told her I couldn't take her in and drove her to a homeless shelter. My life took so many turns after that, that I never thought about her again and yet here she was, with a gun aimed at me. I asked God to forgive me for all my trespasses, expecting this to be my time of death. Ronnie interrupted all my thinking…

    "I thought it was some sort of fate that the

temp agency placed me at the same place of work as you. I was going to actually thank you and ask your forgiveness. I spoke so many negative wishes against you in my time at the shelter, but it took all the good things that happened in my life to make me realize that my steps were still ordered, with or without yours or anyone else's support," she told me while holding the gun steady. "I was so ready to put the animosity behind me and befriend you, but when you didn't even so much as recognize me, I was done with all considerations of it. The more I watched you at work, the more I saw your hypocrisy and I couldn't stand your presence. I would have quit, but I've got goals and I am not letting you or any other person on this planet stop me from achieving them."

"I am sorry for all of it, Ronnie, I really am, and I hope you can find peace even if you can't forgive me," I said earnestly.

"See, you are mistaken. I forgive you but I am not going to keep dealing with you and that will be my peace. But know this, if you keep harassing me at work, or otherwise, I am pressing charges," Ronnie declared.

With that she lowered the gun and invited me to leave. I did as she instructed and felt extreme guilt the whole way home. It is true what the wise ones have said.

Whatever you spend your time meditating on the most will eventually come out of you. There was old business that my spirit still had and I had meditated on so much negative for so many years. It was still coming back to me in different ways so I could properly deal with it.

The next day, I sat at my desk and asked God what to do. I told Him how badly I needed to feel from Him that I was forgiven. As I began to talk to God, I found it wasn't about Him granting me forgiveness, but instead it was about me learning to yield and stay focused to the voice of God. I asked God to use me when I got saved, but through my walk I was focused on what God could do for me instead of how could I serve others. We ask God for spiritual gifts but when awarded them, some of us don't know how to use them. It wasn't for me to attack Ronnie. It was for me to be a walking example of Christ and/or Christianity, pray for her and continue to walk in love in spite of her wrongdoings.

Of course my flesh was kicking and screaming when I got this revelation, because a part of me did not want anything to do with her. However, the statement she made about me being a Christian was quickly brought back to my memory. Obviously she had been watching the Christ in me from day one. I had to swallow my pride and ask her to forgive me; Pride being the keyword in the notion. A lot of God's people miss the mark because of lack of humility. We tend to get in a mindset of being perfect or not wanting to be around people in our circle… or we get so focused on being used or on our individual ministries that we don't slow down enough to be in tune with God.

We do not see any of the work He has for us. How does one become sensitive to the spirit and the needs of others? It's not about you but God. Be truly after God's heart and then you will have a heart for his people. As these realizations came to me, I knew what I would do as a gift to her. I put in my resignation and sent out an apology to all those who were affected by me not being focused on God. I wished them all the best and I started fresh in all areas of life.

Over time, I quietly kept tabs on Ronnie. She finished her education, continued to rise in the ranks at the office, and at some point married a Youth Minister and became a wonderful mother. The last I heard, she and her husband had started a non-profit organization. It is for abused youth to go for safe haven and talk to officers and social workers without the watchful eye of their abusers on them.

They would then be escorted to an emergency foster home until the investigation was completed. I was truly amazed at what she was doing with the Boaz who had found her. She didn't know it, but I was inspired by her and often rallied corporate sponsors and anonymous donors to submit funds to her organization. It wasn't out of guilt that I did it, but respect.

Chapter Nine

Incubus or Succubus

What do you do when you find a guy that becomes the twinkle of your eye? What do you do when you have fear of losing control, because the guy you love is a real butthole? You love to love him and then you hate him constantly, thinking of ways to bait him; not hate him because he doesn't want you, but because he needs taming. See I got a man that's used to women gamin'.

You say to yourself, will he ever change or will he soon become estranged? Estranged, caused to be unloved; I give this man my heart, my body, my mind and soul, but he still sees me as a woman he needs to mold. I am a woman capable of holding my own, but I am not exempt from fears of growing old alone. Maybe one day, before it's too late, I'll meet someone who understands the word helpmate—to walk by my side, love and cherish to death do us part. Does anyone understand that's the key to my heart? Love so divine—this guy is blowing my mind. However, his insecurities keep tearing us apart as he continues to allow the enemy to use him as a dart. I wish he would stand still and allow his heart to be healed. The hurt—the pain—the shame from women playing games.

Lord, where is my Boaz, my man, my lover—my soulmate? The man that has a relationship with You, God… The man that puts his pride and insecurities to the side so he can usher in his bride.

That was one of my musings as I pulled myself together spiritually. I was definitely on the right track, but still not crossing paths with my Boaz. Boaz means in him is strength. To give you a little background, during biblical times Boaz completed Ruth, described in the King James' Bible, Book of Ruth. Completion in my opinion is the same as in the beginning when God made woman of man's flesh. "Bone of bone; flesh of flesh," which makes one.

A lot of us seek Boaz, but fail at our quest. It took all my earlier failures in what seemed like love to understand that we are not supposed to be in pursuit, simply because it is not the design for woman to seek man. The bible says, a man that findeth a wife findeth a good thing. So, in other words, we are supposed to be sought after. Nevertheless, we get twisted as we use our emotions, which can be distorted and take us off course from what God has for us. We focus on the idea of being in love or not lonely, ultimately hooking up with men that are incubus in character. The men are not all bad men, but the strongholds that exist within them make them unstable creatures, making it impossible to connect with his Ruth.

An incubus is a spirit that descends upon sleeping persons:

- A nightmare or burden

- Something that worries, oppresses or depresses others

An incubus is anything that keeps you bound in your mind.

Further readings reveal the incubus as being a spirit or demon thought in medieval times to lie on sleeping persons, especially women, with whom it sought sexual intercourse. As I meditated on the word 'incubus,' I drew additional meaning from in it in its syllabic parts. **I N-CU-BUS.**

IN- Used to indicate inclusion within space, a place or limits

Ladies, who have you allowed into your heart, mind, body and soul? Who have you allowed to penetrate your sacred places, such as your home and bed?

CU- C.U. = Close up

Who have you been close up and personal with?

BUS- The verb usage is to transport or convey. The noun usage is a vehicle equipped with seats for passengers.

Ask yourself, who have you allowed to ejaculate in you? Whose seed are you transporting or bussing around?

Even in my new higher focus, I fell for the game of it. I gave a celibate relationship a go with a man named Caleb. I thought he was everything. In fact, I was the one who asked him out first. I found myself mothering him instead of letting him take the lead. My version of supporting a man was all mixed up. We weren't married or even living together, but I was at his home often. I was cleaning for him, cooking for him, drawing him baths, massaging his feet, paying some of his bills if it seemed that he was behind. Everything I did for him became extravagant.

I found myself thinking that every time he opened his mouth in my direction it was going to be a proposal. I stayed in that loop with Caleb for a long time. I had been in business long enough to see that I had no returns on my investment, but I kept hanging on and making excuses. I couldn't let go of him. I really needed to believe he was the one and I just wasn't being patient. I spoke a lot of negative things to myself in that time, always feeling as though I needed to raise my game in some respect. One day, when he told me not to come over after work because he was sick, I became worried. When I asked what it was, he assured me it was just a cold and there was no need for me to get sick too. I thought to myself that I had not yet cared for him when he was sick and, if I did, maybe it would be the final marker to him that I would make a perfect wife. I got off early and made him a homemade soup. I went to his place and, when he did not come to the door, I put the pot down and used the spare key he kept taped under the window shutter.

As I picked up the pot and walked in, I instantly noticed remnants of sand on the floor. Had he been to the beach? I put the pot down on the coffee table and went down the hall, cautiously, like in a horror movie. I saw a bikini bottom, a halter top, and his trunks… I slowly opened the bedroom door and saw them both sleeping soundly, wrapped in each other's arms, seeming a perfect fit. Just like in a horror movie, I stepped back and tripped up. They woke and he jumped up, asking me what I was doing there.

"I'm sorry, I, I…" Then I ran off.

Who in the world was that? That wasn't me. I would never just run out without a confrontation. What was really going on? Was this a good thing or a bad thing?

He came to my place later that evening and I accepted his apology when he told me about his urges and manly needs. I recalled the celibacy being my big idea, but he had seemed on board. He told me that he didn't think I was going go past a month and that a year had been ridiculous. When I asked him why he didn't just discuss it with me, he said he didn't want to hurt my feelings or run me off. So he did love me! Yep, that is what I told myself when he said that and I was highly disappointed in myself by what happened next. We made love, without a condom, and I let him cum inside me on the exact same day he had sex with her. The next day, I panicked and went to the doctor. He told me not to worry and to call back if I actually had a symptom.

I ended up having symptoms alright. I got pregnant and so did she. I watched him marry her and pretend I never existed. No matter how much I called him or dropped by, he did not answer. By my fourth month of pregnancy, I had already accepted the fact that I was going to be a single mother and decided to focus my attention on the new life in me. My world was rocked when I lost him. He was barely any size at all and would have been everything to me if I had the chance. Crying, I called Caleb to let him know but he was indifferent. He coldly told me it was meant to be that way and offered me no comfort. He hung up and we never spoke again.

I named our baby Isaac and had my own private ceremony in his honor. In the months after, I was a shell of myself, but having learned my lessons, I kept reading the word of God and continued to pray. I knew that Caleb was full of spirits that I needed to remain far from and not be connected to in order to fulfill my purpose.

A lot of us women are the walking dead, or stuck in a trance for a lack of better words; and looking for a way out of the drama. We have allowed different people and spirits to have sexual intercourse with us.

As a result, it has left us empty spiritually, mentally and physically. We have opened sexual domains that have made us lose who we were designed to be. And let me go on record as saying this spirit also exists in women, it is called succubus.

By design men penetrate into all the places inside and women naturally receive. However, a woman can destroy a man with her Delilah spirit—deceit, manipulation and lies, sucking the life out of whom she preys upon, eventually destroying him. Some examples of this destructive behavior are be gold-digging women, emotionally unstable women, women seeking to devour married men… the list goes on. Men contaminate women with their semen as they are called to be leaders over women, and by design it is a woman's nature to follow. This would explain the importance of women being selective and careful of whom they are following. Biblically speaking, you should be following God and allowing him to send you Boaz.

We don't always do that and, since I know the majority of us don't wait for God, I am going to just keep it real. We women are screwing everyone that remotely resembles Boaz. As a result we are being implanted with the seed that the incubus carries. For example:

- Low self-esteem

- Rejection

- Laziness

- Adultery

- Lying

- Anger

And this list can go on as well. The point I am trying to make is that both men and women are allowing draining spirits into their lives. My purpose in sharing all of these details from my life with you with some creative writing is to lead you away from such pitfalls. It women who I had in mind when writing this book, and so I am going to preach to the women, but male readers can surely gain some insight as well.

Have you ever wondered why you just flip the hell out as if you are bipolar or have Tourette's, even though you know these diseases don't exist in your bloodline? One minute you love your incubus man and then you hate him. That's because your ass is sleeping and it is time to wake up. You have allowed him to incubate you. You have allowed your man's spiritual semen to preserve your spiritual eggs until the embryo hatches, but because incubus semen carries so many contaminated fluids you give birth to Leviathan, which would explain your mood swings. Leviathan is not a demon, but a principality. Leviathan posses seven heads which are, according to the Book of Job:

- Haughty eyes

- Swift tongue

- Hands that shed innocent blood

- Heart that devises wicked purpose

- Feet of mischief

- False witnessing

- Discord

The Leviathan spirit is so twisted that it literally will make you believe a lie when the truth is tapping you on the shoulder. Leviathan and incubus joined together kills you mentally and spiritually. Before you know it, your bank accounts are drained, your car is destroyed; the spirit literally corrupts you and doesn't take responsibility for any wrongdoing. The spirit will take you on a guilt trip and, before you know it, you are in over your head pulling a grown man up by his bootstrings while at the same time holding on for dear life.

What do I mean by that? We women meet men who are unstable. They're nice men some of the time, yet we allow ourselves to become attached to the instability and get mad when things don't turn out like we envisioned. So the question is, what do you do about it once the blinders come off? Woman to woman, I will never tell anyone to leave their mate. I can only provide them with information and the choice will respectfully be theirs to make. The only statement I can truly make is, When you are tired of going through it, you will let go.

On the flipside, it doesn't have to be about letting go but about both of you getting on one accord and receiving deliverance from things that have you bound. This brings me to my next topic… both participants in the relationship should consider tracing back their family roots. There is a saying that goes like this: If you want to know whom you are dating, then look at the mother and the father of whom you are dating. Discover what issues exist within the realms of the families; identify the strongholds and general rational curses that are hindering the two of you. Where does this lead the two of you? Two hurt people hooking up to hurt each other, due to the lack of understanding of love, pain and hurt.

    After Caleb, I dated a guy named Sean. I was hurting due to my series of bad relationships and the loss of a child. I was clearly not equipped to start anything new with anyone and, for that matter, neither was he. As you read in earlier chapters, I was caught in a vicious cycle of pain, so I'm sure we can agree I had no business entering into a new relationship without time to heal. The guy I was dating definitely shouldn't have rushed in either, considering he was just as wounded as I was. He had just ended a marriage due to infidelity on the wife's part.

    I was introduced to him by way of his mother when he and I both were in the area for the holidays. I knew his mother from my young adult years. She was psychotic then and is still is now. I should have kept walking and said no thanks, but curiosity about the mysterious man, who magically lived near me at my new home, made me willing to go on a coffee date. He disclosed to me that he wasn't raised by his mother. His grandparents raised him and he actually had no dealings with his mother until his adult years. So I exhaled and said, "Thank goodness he hasn't been tarnished," but I never stopped to think about the buried pain and anger a person carries as a victim of abandonment. After all, I carried it quite heavily for a long time. He was dealing with abandonment from his mother and his ex-wife. All it took was one bad situation that resembled those two people to unleash the pain.

The grandparents instilled the love and values into him which were the parts of his character that drew me to him, but the bottom line is that our genetics and DNA follows us. Our DNA shapes us, but we don't have to succumb to it. We can let God transform us. While dating Sean, there would always be this battle with rage and anger in him. In my opinion, he inherited this from his mother. There is much more I could say about Sean's mother and father as an outsider, reaching back into the history of Sean's immediate family tree, but to protect those I cherish I am unable to disclose in depth information regarding his family.

So, keeping it general, Sean and I dated for an extended period of time but, the deeper the relationship went, the more the unhealed wounds in both us became unstitched. Sean dealt with his issues by drinking and

I dealt with mine through outbursts of rage. I liked to stay and fight it out, whereas he was prone to try to flee whether he was sober or not.

Our relationship was awesome during the good times and bad, which is hard to explain other than that the good times were far more frequent. Even so, I did have reservations with his drinking. As a child, my father was an alcoholic and I saw what that did to our family. So there was always a fear that existed within me when dealing with Sean. When Sean got depressed, he would go out on a drinking binge and I wouldn't see him until the next day. This disturbed me, as this man had proposed to me during our relationship. At that time I wondered, *Can I really enter into a marriage with someone that will keep me up half the night worrying when he goes out on one of these binges?* So, I told him I needed time to think. He respected my need to do so and our relationship continued as usual.

Then one day the unthinkable happened. I got a call from the hospital. There had been a terrible accident. When I arrived, Sean was not alone. He was being treated, but was handcuffed to a bed. Sean had been arrested for drinking and driving. He would be transported to jail as soon as he got treatment for his injuries. I couldn't understand what had led him to drink that night as the whole week had been perfect, but then again, do we ever understand depression and the mind of an alcoholic? Don't get me wrong—I am not judging Sean, but this made me even more scared to enter into a marriage with him. Being with him in that state would be walking the same path that my parents walked.

I am a believer and know that God is a deliverer, but I also acknowledge that God helps those that help themselves and Sean would have to want to be delivered.

Sean was eventually released from jail, but I had forgotten that jail could be made to exist beyond the prison bars. 'Jail on the outside' is what happened next. What Sean didn't realize was that, between the day he was arrested and the day he was sentenced to his terms of probation, the course of the lives that were tied to him was deeply affected. In fact, the course of his whole life changed. There were monthly visits to the Parole Office and a ton of restitution fees to the state that Sean couldn't cover on his own, but those who loved him pitched in to help. In a sense, I hated him for wrecking our lives and resurfacing old memories in me, but I tried to make sense of the blessing in it that changed his behavior.

On the night of the accident, his blood alcohol level was absurd. Not only did he cause other cars to crash into each other, he totaled his own vehicle. It was so crunched up that it didn't make any sense that anyone in it could still be alive. When I asked him about it, Sean stated that he saw his life flash before his eyes in the way that many people describe in near-death experiences. When he learned about all the people he could have hurt by his own death or the deaths of others, he knew he had to change.

    The passionate way he shared his testimony really had me under the belief that he had an intention to change. I still needed to witness consistent action. My emotions were shaky, as I had heard my father utter those words so many times to my mother, my siblings, me, my grandmother, and so on. My love for Sean wanted to have no doubts at all; my love for God wanted to believe that all things are possible, yet it was just one of those easier-said-than-done feelings of life.

    One of the terms of the probation was to have an interlock device placed on his car. What this device does is detect any alcohol levels on the breath before the person is able to start their vehicle. A year went by and Sean hadn't had a drink or an accident of any kind. Our relationship was pretty good, but still strained and slowly headed for disaster. Why? Because I still found myself wondering if the desire for a drink was truly gone, or whether he was just afraid to take a drink because of the scrutiny he was under with the terms of his probation.

I asked myself if I was wrong for feeling this way. The probation still had a great deal of time left on it. I know I have made plenty of mistakes, but I was feeling like the whole thing was a deal-breaker. Sean and I eventually ended up mutually breaking off our relationship. It was just simply too much for me to handle, and it wouldn't have been fair for me to be unforgiving, or enter into a marriage with doubt and distrust. It is out of love, not judgment, that I released him. Even today we are good friends and I have been proud of our relationship with each other—it is authentic and no boundaries are crossed.

So in all that I have provided of myself in this body of work, I know that people would have better, lasting relationships if they deal with that haunting from the inner child. We all have it. It may be at different levels but it is there. This is where a life story takes a turn towards relationship advice and the launch of self-help as a product of experience and the profound shareable lessons learned.

In a nutshell, I will say we all have flaws, but you still should know who you are marrying. Check the background and character traits of a person. Know that, even if there are some negatives in the history, this doesn't disqualify him or her from being a wonderful spouse. Again, I point at myself as an example, but the two of you must be willing to work together to prevent those family curses from disrupting your household.

The two of you must be honest and know the limitations of what you can handle before you step off into a marriage. Sit down and discuss what marriage means to the both of you. Identify the personal strongholds you struggle with, even if it is something that may embarrass you. Talk about it! Why hide it? It eventually will be exposed if you have whorish tendencies, alcoholic tendencies or whatever you may be dealing with. Internally talk about it. This is what true covenant is… being able to expose the issues before you step into a marriage and be delivered from the things that have you bound so you can have a healthy bond. For those who are already married, it's just matter of renewing your vows and tearing down the strongholds. The same principles apply. The way to deal with any type of bondage hindering a relationship is to be mature and deal with it without finger pointing. A structured outcome is the true meaning of a Boaz and Ruth relationship.

Remember Boaz means in him is strength. Does

your man have the power and strength to deal with your demons and denounce them from your life? Or does he incubate them? Does your man understand being head of household? Remember, in the story of Boaz and Ruth, Boaz redeemed Ruth. And for the women, it is pertinent that you know who you are in God so you will recognize the true call of Boaz and not experience the hard life lessons as I did. It important that you, the woman, are stable in the mind and have the spirit of Ruth, which is a meek humble and serving spirit, so when Boaz does arrive you will be capable of treating him like royalty.

    Let your spirit guide your family rather than your mouth and that, my sisters, will be handing Boaz the key to your heart. I know that this will be a hard task for the new-age women to do. I am guilty of this myself. We are so used to being independent women, but remember, anything worth having is hard work. Use wisdom in all things and remember: the key to overcoming every battle is being of one accord.

    Overall, I came to realize that in order for Boaz to find me, he must be delivered himself and continually draw strength from God to transfer to me and any children we have. As women, we have a tendency to want to be rescued by a knight in shining armor, figuratively speaking. In this book, I introduced you to several of them, including a faux Joan of Arc. You can not be lead by anyone who isn't guided by the Holy Spirit and the more you grow, the more you have discernment who is and who is not.

We women go from relationship to relationship seeking that perfect one. We spend the majority of our time trying to shape and mold a man into what we want him to be. The more I come into a deeper relationship with God, the more I begin to understand that in order for Boaz to come I have to know God's meaning of love, instead of wondering if each man I meet is Boaz. If you are patient and request clear visibility when he arrives, you won't have to wonder.

Also, Boaz should be secure in the things of God securing him in who you are called to be in God. This releases him to love you unconditionally. There are so many men that don't know who they are because of the pain and lack of forgiveness they carry. Their minds are trapped in their past, making it hard for them to step into their future destinies. Our men have been conditioned to destroy, but a strong man of God doesn't believe the lies of the enemy, rather declares life over himself and walks in victory. Women, if you encounter a broken man, impart love into him; don't tear him down even more. Women often complain about their husbands or how their male friends treat them, but I ask you this question:

Are we setting examples such as speaking life and praying for our men?

Your catharsis will come and so will his, through dedicated prayer for you both.

In a world where challenges have become a trend, consider yourself challenged to 30 Days of Prayer after having read this book. Many books will provide you with prayers to say but I will not do so. Prayers are deeply personal and should have the same individuality that we do as people. So I will not provide you with the words to say. Here, you will find scriptures to meditate on so that you may be guided to your interpretations, realizations, words to share with God. My only recommendation is to always start out with gratitude.

Chapter Ten
The obvious concerning you…

As you've read, life has had it out for me since the beginning. I've existed in pieces. The notion of wholeness was a foreign notion. Everytime I thought I pieced myself togehter, life revealed just how fragile I was. Around each corner there was a speeding wrecking ball with my name on it. I'm convinced my birthmark must be a target.

True healing entered my life when I started APPLYING the Word of God to my life. The constant chaos ceased, and peace was presented. I found myself in the stillness and became whole once I submitted fully to God.

On your road to healing submit your pieces to the potter's wheel. Allow God to mend and mold your heart and soul. Some situations scar our soul. There's only one that can perform that type of surgery.

Prepare to be "The Virtuous Wife"
(NKJV) (Proverbs 10-31)

Day 1 *[You Are Not a Succubus and Can Be Trusted Above Any Other. You Are Filled with Goodness and Wisdom with Only the Best of Intentions for Him.]*:

10 Who can find a virtuous wife? For her worth is far above rubies. 11 The heart of her husband safely trusts her; So he will have no lack of gain. 12 She does him good and not evil, All the days of her life. 13 She seeks wool and flax, And willingly works with her hands. 14 She is like the merchant ships, She brings her food from afar.

Day 2 *[You Are Diligent and Dedicated to the Cause of Creating Order in Your Home. You Are Willing to Go Above and Beyond the Call of Duty by Strength of God and Are Selfless in Random Acts of Kindness]*: 15 She also rises while it is yet night, And provides food for her household, And a portion for her maidservants. 16 She considers a field and buys it; From her profits she plants a vineyard. 17 She girds herself with strength, And strengthens her arms. 18 She perceives that her merchandise is good, And her lamp does not go out by night. 19 She stretches out her hands to the distaff, And her hand holds the spindle. 20 She extends her hand to the poor, Yes, she reaches out her hands to the needy

Day 3 *[You Plan for Good Times and Bad, So You Constantly Make Sound Preparations So Basic Needs Are Met During Those Times. She Too Is a Contributor to the Financial Wellbeing of the Household yet Remains Aware of the Importance of Allowing Her Husband to Serve as Lead Provider.]*:

21 She is not afraid of snow for her household, For all her household is clothed with scarlet. 22 She makes tapestry for herself; Her clothing is fine linen and purple. 23 Her husband is known in the gates, When he sits among the elders of the land. 24 She makes linen garments and sells them, And supplies sashes for the merchants.

Day 4 *[She Is Humble and Unyielding in Her Hard Work, Careful in Advisement, and Demonstrates*

Kindness in All Her Actions.]:

25 Strength and honor are her clothing; She shall rejoice in time to come. 26 She opens her mouth with wisdom, And on her tongue is the law of kindness. 27 She watches over the ways of her household, And does not eat the bread of idleness.

Day 5 [*Maintain Focus on Your Purpose as Given to You by God and You Will Be Rewarded by Him. People in Your Life Won't Be Able to Dismiss All that You Have Done
over Time.*]:

28 Her children rise up and call her blessed; Her husband also, and he praises her: 29 "Many daughters have done well, But you excel them all." 30 Charm is deceitful and beauty is passing, But a woman who fears the Lord, she shall be praised. Give her of the fruit of her hands, And let her own works praise her in the gates.

Concerning Him…
(Scripture Selections from theodysseyonline.com, taken from the NKJV)

Remember, your Boaz does not have to be present in your life yet for you to pray earnestly for him. You may not have met him yet, but he is out there and always in need of prayer from his Ruth.

Day 6 *[His Surrender to God's Will]*:

I, therefore, the prisoner of the Lord, beseech you to walk worthy of the calling with which you were called, with all lowliness and gentleness, with long suffering, bearing with one another in love. (Ephesians 4:1- 2)

Day 7 *[Blessings and Dedication at His Job]*:

Do you see a man who excels in his work? He will stand before kings; He will not stand before unknown men. (Proverbs 22:29)

Day 8 [*God Is His Source of Guidance and Strength in Hard Times*]:

God is our refuge and strength, A very present help in trouble.(Psalm 46:1)

Day 9 [*He Always Demonstrates Integrity*]:

The integrity of the upright will guide them, But the perversity of the unfaithful will destroy them.(Proverbs 11:3)

Day 10 [*He Is Not Attentive to Temptation*]:

No temptation has overtaken you except such as is common to man; but God is faithful, who will not allow you to be tempted beyond what you are able, but with the temptation will also make the way of escape, that you may be able to bear it.(1 Corinthians 10:13)

Day 11 [*He Demonstrates Goodwill and Kind Acts*]:

He who gives to the poor will not lack, But he who

hides his eyes will have many curses. (Proverbs 28:27)

Day 12 *[He Provides through Sound Financial Management]*:

No servant can serve two masters; for either he will hate the one and love the other, or else he will be loyal to the one and despise the other. You cannot serve God and mammon. (Luke 16:13)

Day 13 *[He Succeeds through Awareness of God's Plan and Recognizes When What He Is Doing Has Little to Do with God's Intentions]:*

For I know the thoughts that I think toward you, says the Lord, thoughts of peace and not of evil, to give you a future and a hope. (Jeremiah 29:11)

Day 14 *[He Places All Matters in Life to Prayer]*:

Rejoice always, pray without ceasing.(1 Thessalonians 5:17)

Day 15 *[He Has True Discernment through God and Makes Excellent Decisions as a Result]*:

If any of you lacks wisdom, let him ask of God, who gives to all liberally and without reproach, and it will be given to him.(James 1:5)

Day 16 *[He Is Not Spiritually Stagnant and Constantly Seeks More Wisdom]*:

And this I pray, that your love may abound still more and more in knowledge and all discernment, that you may approve the things that are excellent, that you may be sincere and without offense till the day of Christ. (Philippians 1:9-10)

Day 17 *[He Relies on God's Teachings on How Each of Us Can Be Great Spouses]*:

Wives, submit to your own husbands, as to the Lord. For the husband is head of the wife, as also Christ is head of the church; and He is the Savior of the body. (Ephesians 5:22-33)

Day 18 *[If He Has Fears, He Will Turn Them over to God]*:

The Lord is on my side; I will not fear. What can man do to me? (Psalm 118:6)

Day 19 *[He Will Be Fully Aware When His Purpose Is Revealed to Him and Stick to It in Respect of God and His Design]*:

And we know that all things work together for good to those who love God, to those who are the called according to His purpose.(Romans 8:28)

Day 20 *[He Will Be Focused on Wellness of Mind, Body, and Spirit]*:

All things are lawful for me, but all things are not helpful. All things are lawful for me, but I will not be brought under the power of any. (1 Corinthians 6:12)

Day 21 *[He Will Know Where His Spiritual Strength*

Comes from and Demonstrate It through Word and Actions]:

Lord is my strength and my shield; My heart trusted in Him, and I am helped; Therefore my heart greatly rejoices, And with my song I will praise Him. (Psalm 28:7)

Day 22 *[He Is Surrounded by Upright People Who Will Build Him Up, Not Take Him Off of His Spiritual Path]:*

He who walks with wise men will be wise, but the companion of fools will be destroyed. (Proverbs 13:20)

Day 23 *[He Boldly Supports and Shares the Word of God]:*

Then Paul dwelt two whole years in his own rented house, and received all who came to him, preaching the kingdom of God and teaching the things which concern the Lord Jesus Christ with all confidence, no one forbidding him. (Acts 28:30-31)

Day 24 *[He Will Be Growth-Minded, Pray Consistently, and Read His Bible Daily]:*

You therefore, beloved, since you know this beforehand, beware lest you also fall from your own steadfastness, being led away with the error of the wicked; but grow in the grace and knowledge of our Lord and Savior Jesus Christ. To Him be the glory both now and forever. Amen. (2 Peter 3:17-18)

Day 25 *[That He Will Not Abuse His Wisdom and Be Willing to Learn from Other Devotees]:*

The fear of the Lord is the instruction of wisdom, And before honor is humility. (Proverbs 15:33)

Day 26 *[He Will Have a Patient Spirit and Act in the Interest of Peace]:*

Therefore let us pursue the things which make for peace and the things by which one may edify another.

(Romans 14:19)

Day 27 *[He Will Be Forgiving of People, Including Himself, for Past and Present Occurrences that Gave Him Pain or Disappointment]:*

And be kind to one another, tenderhearted, forgiving one another, even as God in Christ forgave you. (Ephesians 4:32)

Day 28 *[That He Will Keep His Heart Guarded from Things Meant to Distract Him from God]:*

Keep your heart with all diligence, For out of it spring the issues of life.(Proverbs 4:23)

Day 29 *[That He Understands that, No Matter What is Happening in His Life, God Has Planned a Glorious Future]:*

For He remembered His holy promise, And Abraham His servant. He brought out His people with joy, His chosen ones with gladness. He gave them the lands of the Gentiles, And they inherited the labor of the nations, That they might observe His statutes And keep His laws. Praise the Lord! (Psalm 105: 42-45)

Day 30 *[That He Will Value Your Relationship with Each Other]:*

Husbands, love your wives, just as Christ also loved the church and gave Himself for her, that He might sanctify and cleanse her with the washing of water by the word, that He might present her to Himself a glorious church, not having spot or wrinkle or any such thing, but that she should be holy and without blemish. So husbands ought to love their own wives as their own bodies; he who loves his wife loves himself. For no one ever hated his own flesh, but nourishes and cherishes it, just as the Lord does the church. (Ephesians 5:25- 29)

May your meditation and prayers lead you to the place of fulfillment and peace that God designed for you since before you were born; all you have to do is be willing to connect with Him and allow Him to be the leader of your life. A change will come.

Pieced Together

Meet Who Pieced Me Together

Jesus rained amazing grace in my life and I'm blessed I didn't have an umbrella. You too can receive the freeing power of salvation. Release every bond, every chain, every negative mindset. Submit your wounds to Jehovah Rappha, *God who heals*. The best relationship I've ever had is with Jesus. It was the easiest to start, I will like you to meet him.

Piece one: God Loves YOU and offers a wonderful PLAN for YOUR life.

- John 3:16
- John 10:10

Piece Two: We are sinful and separated from God. Therefore, we cannot know and experience God's love and plan for our life

- We are sinful: Romans 3:23

- We are seperated: Romans 6:23

Piece Three: Jesus Christ is God's ONLY provision for our sin. Through Jeus we can know and experience God's love and plan for our life.

- He DIED in OUR place: Romans 5:8
- He Rose from THE DEAD: 1 Corinthians 15:3-6
- He is the ONLY way to God: John 14:16

Piece Four: WE must individually receive Jesus Christ as Savior and Lord; then we can know and experience God's love and plan for our lives.

- We MUST receive Christ: John 1:12
- We receive Christ through FAITH: Ephesians 2:8-9
- When we receive Christ, we experience a new birth: John 3:1-8

I wanted you to see what the Lord has to say about your life for yourself. Salvation is a prayer away

The Prayer Of Salvation

"Lord Jesus, I need you. Thank You for dying on the cross for my sins. I open the door of my life and receive you as my Savior and Lord. Thank You for forgiving my sins and giving me eternal life. Make me the kind of person YOU want me to be. In Jesus' name, AMEN!!"

Congratulations you have received the most important piece of your life, SALVATION Your eternal address is in Heaven! Important pieces to hold are prayer and studying the Word of God as you Journey Back To You!

Bonus

Exclusive Excerpt From 'Nightmare On Mr. 68 St.'

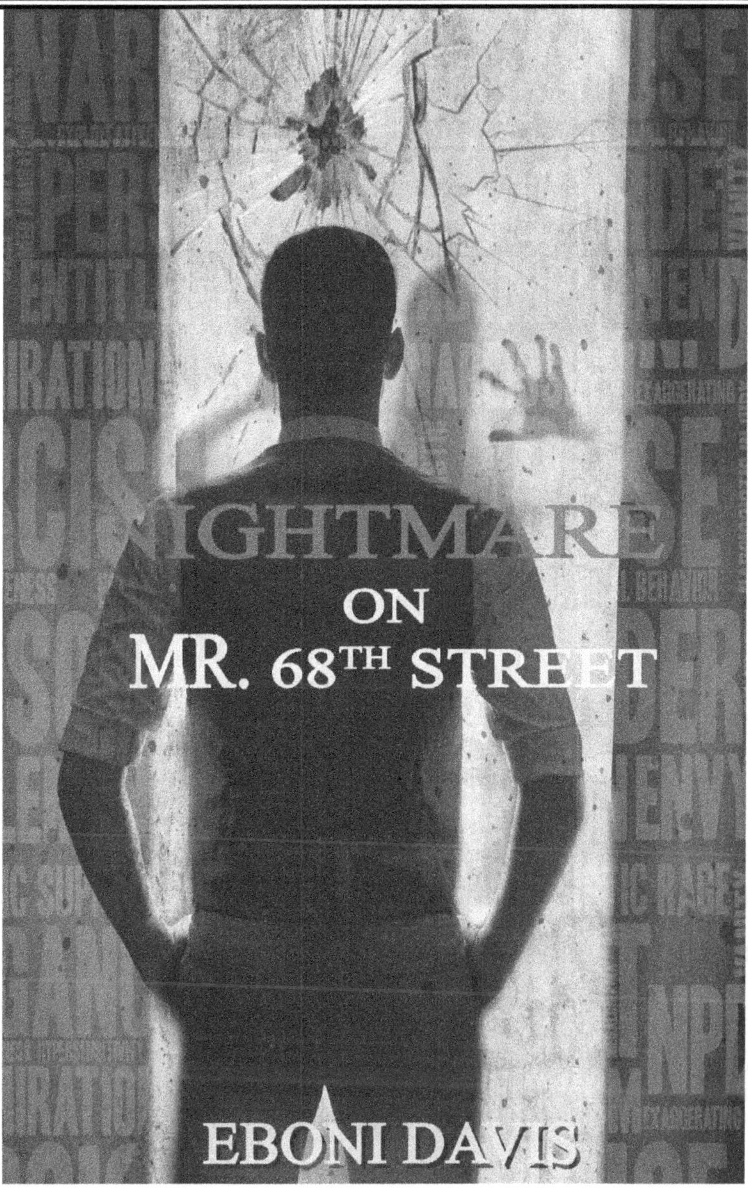

I have a light in me. It draws two types of people, lighters and snuffers. The lighters have the same flame, often making me shine brighter than before. The snuffers attempt to deprive me of oxygen until there is no trace of light left. This is the story of time when I could not tell the difference between a lighter and a snuffer. I had to learn to reignite my own flame.

We met when I was in my early twenties. I call him Mr. 68 because that is his age. He is 22 years older than me. He always played a leadership or helper role in my life. In over twenty years of knowing him, I had never been intimate with him. He was a real friend. I grew to love Mr. 68 just for being so kind to me. Our friendship only became strained when I got married. Five years went by and I did not reconnect with him until after my marriage went bad. I reached out to Mr. 68 because I truly missed him being apart of my life.

The difference at this point was the noticeably strong attraction to each other. I called it a soul-tie. We crossed over from friendship to a lot more. I learned so much from Mr. 68 when it was new and fun. As the years went on things became toxic and the relationship went awry. I discovered the relationship was built on lies. There were red flags that I missed or chose not to acknowledge. It's kind of funny how I never really knew him until I dated him. The twenty-plus years I knew him, did not reveal the monster that existed within. I was blinded because he was that friend who was only a phone call away, full of wisdom laced conversation, and a helper that always came to the rescue.

Once we began dating I did feel deep down in my heart that something was not quite right about Mr. 68 but I ignored my inner feelings. The more the relationship progressed, I still felt empty. I had to ask myself why? I later found out he was married and not truthful about many things. I guess you're probably saying you were friends with him for over twenty-two years and you never knew he was married? That just it. He never presented Himself as a married man.

I had always seen him live the life of a single man. I had watched this man have full- blown relationships with women and reside in the same residence with them. I never knew of a wife! As we continued to build our relationship, Mr. 68 became disgruntled for no reason. At the time that we met, I was very fragile and his aloof sporadic behavior would often leave me with feelings of confusion. He would cut his phone off or block my calls and literally become a ghost for days at a time when he chose not to be bothered with me. I accepted not knowing where Mr. 68 lived. I accepted the lies the foundation was built on. I accepted the manipulation. I accepted the narcissistic sociopath behavior of someone that presented himself to my family, friends, and the public as a saint. The reality is Mr. 68 was double-minded, two-faced and living a double life. He is a man of hypocrisy, duality, secrets, and dishonesty. I didn't know it. I was lost in it.

"Nightmare on Mr. 68th Street" is what I sometimes call my experience with his other side. At times it felt as if he would go out of his way to ruin a special time for me. He would ruin special events of importance to me such as vacations, birthdays, holidays, etc. It started small and that is partly why it was missed. I remember traveling to Padre Island for my birthday.

When we got there to celebrate, there was no real celebration. All Mr. 68 wanted to do was work. He brought his laptop with him and I was thinking, *Wow he could not give up a weekend to celebrate with me?*

When I questioned him about it, he went into a rage and shouted at me, "I never wanted to come on this stupid trip anyway! I only drove down here because this was something that you wanted to do!"

Then there was the time that we traveled to Atlanta, Georgia and Washington, DC. Those trips were filled with spikes of happiness and pure chaos. Mr. 68 had severe periodic mood swings.

At times things were great. We would be happy for three or four months, and then he would get angry, vicious, stop talking to me or threaten me in some sort of way. Looking back, the first time it happened was the red flag and I chose to overlook it since it was in the first 3 months of our relationship.

He would make it his personal vendetta to ruin my happiness. What I mean by ruin is, Mr. 68 would pick fights rather than communicate with me. He brooded over small things. Mr. 68 wanted my life to be all about his life. He brainwashed me into completing projects that seemed to be for the betterment of myself but had an underlying agenda of benefiting him. I won't lie and say Mr. 68 ever made me give up on my dreams. As a matter of fact, he was my biggest cheerleader, as long as he was in control.

Whenever I stepped out of the bounds of his control I was verbally attacked, belittled, and sometimes physically abused. His favorite slogan was *"I control my environment and everything in it."* Eventually, anything that I had going outside of him would be poisoned, taken away from me, or redirected. I can still hear his voice saying to me, *"Why do you always feel obligated to join or be apart of someone else's shit. Get your own shit going. I'm trying to make you be more like me you need to be more like me."* i.e. I do not become a part of anything that I cannot control or lead. If I ain't running the show then I ain't a part of it and you need to have that same attitude.

    He put down my personal ideas, talked about my friends, and slowly before I ever realized it, I was isolated. Mr. 68 knew exactly where and how to emotionally strike so that it would hurt and damage me.

www.ingramcontent.com/pod-product-compliance
Lightning Source LLC
Chambersburg PA
CBHW060358190426
43198CB00052B/2105